The experts praise Rick Wilber's
Writer's Handbook for Editing and Revision!

At last! A writing book that acknowledges one of the great secrets of the craft—that the most interesting and important work takes place during the rewrite. Rick Wilber provides sound, time-tested tips on how to discover what's wrong with your own story—and what could be better with it. What's especially useful is the collection of before-and-after drafts.

Professor Patrick Clinton
Medill School of Journalism
Northwestern University

Writer's Handbook for Editing and Revision . . . is a valuable reference that should be on every writer's desk. The section on "Your Writing and the Internet" is especially helpful to those of us who grew up before the computer age. In discussing legal matters and marketing, it adds an important dimension to the act of revision not often found in books of this kind.

Professor Mary Gay Haldeman
Writing Center
Massachusetts Institute of Technology

A great guide for beginning writers, built out of the experience and advice of many veteran writers and editors.

William Keenan, Jr.
Editor
Selling Magazine

(Continued)

Good writing is not simply the product of some capricious creative tempest gusting through the gray matter. It is a process that includes disciplined self-editing, revision and more revision. . . . Beginning writers, or even the most grizzled hacks, can learn much from Rich Wilber's *Writer's Handbook for Editing and Revision.* Wilber has managed to condense decades of insight about writing into a well-written, easy-to-use book that every serious writer should have within arm's reach.

Ronald E. Yates
Financial Writer
Chicago Tribune

A real find. . . . All the fundamental rules of good editing, as well as innovative chapters on query letters and marketing, Internet freelancing, copyright concerns, and editor relationships. Wilber's *Writer's Handbook for Editing and Revision* gives a pro's take on the aesthetics and business of writing—and supports every rule with loads of quotes from seasoned writers.

Catherine Merrill
Associate Professor
Department of Writing and Literature
Johnson State College

The fact that this book's title contains a small lie is excellent news for students, writers and their teachers, for this is a fine guide to *Writing* as well as to "Editing and Revision." It's loaded with common-sense and easy-to-follow drafting and redrafting exercises; offers over-the-shoulder advice in a friendly and straightforward voice; and calls for a wide variety of successful authors to share their stories of writing and rewriting for satisfaction and profit.

John Calderazzo
Professor, English Department
Colorado State University

(Continued)

Rick Wilber's *Writer's Handbook for Editing and Revision* is an excellent toolbox for disassembling your story and putting it back together the right way. Although directed specifically toward beginning journalists, there is valuable advice here for any kind of writer, fact or fiction. Wilber's step-by-step approach helps you ease into useful self-criticism and the systematic repair of your first drafts.

Examples throughout the text make for clarity and easy reading, and the appendix, showing first drafts and published versions of complete articles, is especially valuable.

Professor Joe Haldeman
Program in Writing and Humanistic Studies
Massachusetts Institute of Technology

Rick Wilber's *The Writer's Handbook for Editing and Revision* is simply marvelous: filled with realistic, useful advice and practical exercises to home editing and rewriting skills. This is a book for every writer, from hopeful novice to crusty veteran.

Ben Bova, Author
Former Editor of *Omni* magazine

The Writer's Handbook for Editing & Revision

Rick Wilber

Printed on recyclable paper

NTC *Publishing Group*
Lincolnwood, Illinois USA

Dedication

To Robin, Samantha and Rich,
whose love and support make all the writing
(and the revising) possible.

Library of Congress Cataloging-in-Publication Data

Wilber, Rick, 1948–
    The writer's handbook for editing and revision / Rick Wilber.
        p.   cm.
    Includes index.
    ISBN 0-8442-5916-0 (pbk. : alk. paper)
    1. Editing—Handbooks, manuals, etc.   I. Title.
PN162.W55   1996
808'.027—dc20   96-12973
                                                                          CIP

6 7 8 9 0 VP 9 8 7 6 5 4 3 2 1

Contents

Acknowledgments

This book owes a considerable debt to all those who helped me learn the art and craft of writing and rewriting. William G. Ward at Southern Illinois University-Edwardsville guided my early steps and convinced me I had the skill for this career. Martin Quigley, Joe Hempen, Michael Doran Rudman, Hal Waters, Roberta Bosse—I learned much from them all and thank them for sharing their knowledge and skill.

There is also a long list of writers and editors I've worked with over the years whose advice and guidance was invaluable in my writing this book, including Tom Seals of the *Wichita Eagle*, Dr. Randy Miller at the University of South Florida's School of Mass Communications, and *Tampa Tribune* writers and editors Martha Durrance, Janice Hall, Judy Hill, and Rick Schuerman.

I have always found that I learn as much from my teaching as the students do. In helping them learn to edit and revise their own work I continually discover new elements of the writing craft myself. I owe all the many students over the years a special thanks, and am especially grateful to the Magazine Feature Writing and Advanced Reporting classes of 1995–1996 for their help and patience.

Dr. Edward Jay Friedlander, director of the School of Mass Communications at the University of South Florida, has been extremely supportive of my writing in general, and of this book in particular, and I thank him for that support.

I especially thank the editors and writers whose work I've discussed in this handbook, including the very promising young journalist D. Quentin Wilber III, as well as Sherry Long, Jeannette Batz, the very talented husband and wife writing team of Greg and Lisa Couch, Joe Bargmann, Sarah Beavers, Lynne McChristian, Trudy Thompson-Rice, Jennifer Wittwer, Jonathan Cullimore, the late Murray Cox, and Lloyd Eby.

Writing and revising and then revising some more takes time. I owe a deep debt of gratitude to my family for supporting my work over the years and especially for helping with this handbook. My lovely and talented wife Robin, our delightful daughter Samantha and my hard-working son Rich all contributed to this handbook with their advice and support.

Finally, a special note of thanks is due Rich Hagle, my editor at NTC, whose gentle prodding and sharp eye kept me, and this book, on track toward publication. All writers should be lucky enough to have an editor as capable, energetic and as supportive as Rich.

Introduction

It's nearly midnight, and you've just finished a magazine piece that you've been working on for weeks. The research and interviewing went well, the writing has gone smoothly, and now, after hours of hard work at your computer keyboard, you finally type the last few words, save the file, and sit back with a satisfied smile.

There, you think. It's done.

Tomorrow you'll do a quick run-through with the software's spell-checker, print the story, and send it off in the mail where some enlightened editor will surely figure it's just right and buy it.

After years of talking about it, you think, this time you've really done it. You've written your story and you're on your way.

Ah, wouldn't it be nice if that were so? But what most veteran writers will tell you, quite rightly, is that finishing that first draft of the story doesn't mean you're done. It means only that you're done with the first draft.

For it is in the hard work of revising that you'll take that first draft and turn it into a truly remarkable story. Whether you're a beginning freelancer, a long-time veteran newspaper or magazine writer, a public relations writer, or someone in the business world writing a memo, revising is a major key to successful communication.

That's what this book is all about. What we'll try to do here is give you some advice on how to recognize a story's deficiencies and fix them.

This book deals with the basic elements of presentation, style and grammar, as well as more complex issues of story structure and the fine-tuning that comes from understanding pacing, voice, tone and subtext.

The book discusses legal and ethical issues as well as the business side of writing and editing. You will find some important basic information on libel law, ethics for writers and editors, and copyright protection. There is a chapter on how to work productively with an editor, and a chapter that discusses the digital future for writers and editors. I've even included some tips on marketing your story once you have it ready for submission.

To write this book I've interviewed writers and editors from around the country. They contributed their thoughts and, in some cases, their work. I've included some of my own work, too, taking advantage of a long career in editing and writing nonfiction for newspapers and magazines. As I point out in the book, working as an editor on someone else's copy is good for the writer in you.

The focus, though, throughout this book is on editing and revising your own stories, and it is organized to help you do that. This book should prove useful to you in two ways. First, reading through it should give you a good idea of the importance of revision and a solid understanding of some techniques for revising. Second, the book's organization should make it useful for you for years to come, allowing you to quickly find relevant information when you need advice on revising a particular story.

One of the interesting things I learned in researching and writing this book is how much of writing is *not* a conscious effort on the part of most writers. Most of the writers I've talked to for this and other books aren't very aware of the process of writing while they are doing it. Writing, for most writers, seems to be a natural process.

But when they are revising, things change. And that's what Chapter 1 is all about, the writer's two minds. Read on.

1

Your Editing Mind

Most writers truly enjoy the writing process. Beginning writers and long-time veterans alike know the secret joy of creation, the satisfaction that comes from turning notes and thoughts into something tangible, a written artifact of fiction or nonfiction, a story.

Certainly there are times when the writing comes hard, when every word seems difficult to find. There is no question that the hours of research and interviewing that go into a story before you ever write the first word is demanding, difficult work.

But you know you are becoming a writer when you focus so much on the writing process that time slips away from you and you lose yourself in the story. On those days you sometimes look up and find that two or three hours have gone by as if they were minutes.

That is your writing mind at work; the inventive, creative part of yourself that takes all the input from your research and interviewing and mixes it up with your vocabulary, your education, the books and magazines and newspapers you have read over the years—all those things that comprise your knowledge—to produce word after word, sentence after sentence, paragraph after paragraph, until there is, at last, a story.

Your Creative Mind and Your Editing Mind

It is a marvelous, satisfying thing, being able to create something from nothing.

But there is a problem—one overlooked by too many struggling beginners and even the occasional veteran who can't seem to break into bigger markets.

The creative writer's mind, you see, can be brilliant at conjuring up sterling prose, dazzling in its ability to meet a seemingly impossible deadline, radiant in its capacity to produce page after page of copy with the potential to entertain and inform a reading public. And yet, unfortunately, your creative writer's mind is usually a poor editor.

More likely than not your remarkably creative writer's mind is not particularly good at paying attention to the details, to the rules that govern the writing game.

These rules are critical, because without them we writers couldn't converse with our readers. If we didn't all agree on some basic elements of grammar, structure, and style we wouldn't share the language that permits us to communicate.

All too often, the writing mind, while inventive and creative, spells poorly, can't figure out which words to capitalize, gets sloppy with transitions and structure, and is wordy to the point of boredom.

Someone has to fix these language problems and turn that flawed early draft of a story into a professional, publishable piece.

You want to be that someone. Somehow you have to turn your creative writer's mind into something more ruthless. The mystic who produced that prose has to become a sharp-eyed editor who can find the right spot for each comma and correctly spell *accommodate*. You must learn to ruthlessly cut away the excess and the redundancies that slow the story's pace and bog the reader down in irrelevant detail.

Call it your editing mind, the one that spells better than your writing mind and usually has a much better idea of when and where to capitalize and just how to connect one paragraph with the next.

You must cultivate that editing mind if you're going to succeed as a writer.

Many people edit for a living. Newspapers sometimes have dozens of people whose job it is to fix, change, trim, and otherwise make publishable the daily stories turned in by the paper's reporters.

Magazines, too, have editors whose job it is to work with a writer's material until it is in shape for publication. Indeed, many magazines take the editing task so seriously they have an entry-level position for fact-checkers, beginning editors whose job it is to question every detail in a story. (You can read more about fact-checkers and publication editors in Chapter 8.)

But unless you are a staff writer for a magazine or a newspaper, you probably don't have that kind of regular editing support. You have to find ways to be your own editor.

Even if you *are* a staffer, the wise writer knows that the cleaner and smoother your copy is when it gets to the editor's desk, the greater the likelihood that your story will appear in print in the same shape it was when you submitted it.

Editors, after all, are in the business of editing. They look for mistakes, and they often think that sloppy writing indicates sloppy reporting and a generally sloppy mind. Little mistakes add up, in their minds, to a lack of trust in your work. That lack of trust can lead to a heavy editing hand when the editors work on your story.

What you need to do, then, whether you are a freelancer out on your own or a staff writer who can count on editing help, is learn how to get in the right mind to edit and revise your own copy. You need to learn to switch readily from the writing mind to the editing mind. You need to learn how to see and correct the mistakes you have made before they get to an editor's desk.

A large part of this change is mental. Certainly you need to train yourself in the necessary tools of grammar, style, and structure, or find resources where you can look them up. But yñou also need to train yourself to see the story as if you were the editor seeing it for the first time, ready to be informed and entertained and anxious to find any mistakes or weaknesses before the piece gets into print.

Here are some techniques for finding that editing mind, and how a variety of writers and editors use those techniques:

Techniques for "Changing Your Mind"

Walk Away

Trudy Thompson-Rice has the typical writer's love/hate relationship with deadlines. A Phoenix-based freelance writer for consumer magazines and public relations publications, Thompson-Rice says "When I'm on deadline is usually when I do my best work. Having that deadline pressing down really focuses your attention."

In fact, like a lot of journalism-trained writers, Thompson-Rice admits that without a deadline's approach she sometimes can't find that writing mind. "If I give myself the luxury of too much time, the story seems dead, has no life," she says.

But writing to deadline carries some real risks for the writer. It is all too easy under that kind of pressure to make mistakes that a thoughtful, careful edit and revision process would catch and correct.

For this reason, Thompson-Rice, deadline pressure and all, tries to make sure that she builds in enough time to walk away from her story, then come back to it later when she can take a fresh look.

"For me," she says, "it's important to let a story cool off for a while, give it some time to sit, either in the computer or in my briefcase in hard-copy form. Then when I look back at it I see things I wouldn't see if Federal Express were standing at my door and I was ripping it out of the printer."

Practice the same sort of patience with your story, despite the temptation to celebrate the completion of the first draft by mailing it right out.

For stories with close deadlines, an overnight cooling is best and at least a few hours is crucial. For stories with more distant deadlines, or for something you are writing on speculation that has no real deadline at all, a few days or even a week or more can be very useful.

Change Your Context

Unfortunately, sometimes you may not have even those crucial few hours to leave the story alone. Lynne McChristian, a public relations writer and editor in Florida, also prefers to get away from a story so she can see it fresh, but there are many occasions when she simply doesn't have the time.

"Sure, I like to be able to wait a day or two before coming back to a story I've written. Then you can really see your mistakes and correct them. The story just looks different to me by then," she says.

When she doesn't have that time, which seems to happen more and more these days, she tries a different trick to allow herself to see the story with fresh eyes.

"One thing I try to do is change the story's context. I'll print it out, for instance, so that I'm working with hard copy instead of seeing it again on the screen where I created it."

Moving around the office helps, too. She sits somewhere else to edit and tries to pretend, in an interesting sort of way, that she is someone else.

The whole point, says McChristian, is that "I have to edit my own copy and do my own revisions and do it all rather quickly. Like a lot of places, we're trying to do more with fewer people. This means I have to find a way to almost *be* someone else when I'm editing. Changing the context does that for me."

You can see how effective this technique can be by trying an experiment with your next story. Once you finish the first draft, go through the story quickly on your computer screen, trying to catch any mistakes or problems.

Then print the story out, walk into a different room, and go through the piece again, this time on the hard copy. If you find mistakes now—and you are quite likely to do so—then you will recognize why McChristian goes to the trouble of changing her context when she edits her own copy.

Read It Aloud

Lisa Couch, a public relations writer and editor in Wichita, Kansas, usually doesn't have much time either. What she has found useful is to finish the piece, walk away for only a few minutes, and then return to the story and read it aloud. "Reading it out loud not only allows me to hear how the story sounds, it also slows down my reading of it. If I stumble over something I'll know it's a little awkward or the tone of it isn't what I want," she says.

Greg Couch, Lisa's husband, is a sportswriter for the *Wichita Eagle*. He covers college sports, and often writes to deadline. But even there he has learned, like Lisa, "that it works for me to read a story over out loud half a dozen times before I turn it in."

Line Edit

Another technique that Lisa Couch uses, and one that is particularly useful for beginning writers as well as for veterans, is to force herself to read through the story line by line after she has finished the first draft.

"What I do with my own work as a proofreading tool is put a piece of paper under each line as I read through the hard copy. This forces me to see just what's on that line and not jump ahead, where I might miss something."

A similar technique that you might find useful is to put a dot at the end of each line as you read it. Like the piece of paper Lisa Couch uses to hide the rest of her copy, this will force you to slow down and pay attention to the editing job at hand.

This technique will help you catch grammar and style errors that otherwise might slip by. The important thing to remember is to not put the dot at the end of a line until you are convinced that the line is clean.

Trim the Fat

One of the most important things you need to be able to do in the revision process is to cut. It is not easy to slice away the words you have created, but it is a very necessary part of writing professionally. Much more often than not it greatly improves the story.

If you are a staff writer for a magazine or newspaper, or if you have a contract for your story, you may feel comfortable writing long on purpose for the first draft, knowing that a great deal of cutting is yet to come.

"I usually try to submit a long first draft to my editors," says Joe Bargmann, senior editor at *Seventeen* magazine and an award-winning writer as well. "I think that the editors really appreciate getting the whole picture first, and then we can take it from there, cutting it down."

Jeannette Batz, a writer in St. Louis, would agree. "What I tend to do is write as long as I think any editor could ever want, because it's easier to cut than it is to go back later and add in and weave in new material."

These writers are able to count on an editor's help to trim their stories. You will most likely have to do it yourself.

There are good reasons for this kind of ruthless cutting. For one thing, a typical magazine or newspaper has limited space. (Interestingly, this classic limitation of print publications changes utterly for on-line versions. Read about this important change in Chapter 9.)

It is worth noting that Batz, like most writers, thinks that the trimmed-down version of her story is every bit as good a piece as the longer, earlier draft.

For her story on ADD (See Appendix G), she admits, "I knew when I turned it in that it had a lot of extra information. I wrote it at the max, knowing that the editor would take out anything he thought was too much detail."

Lisa Couch says she discovered the merits of tight writing, and editing hard to make a story tight, when she was in college.

"I was editor for the school paper at the University of Colorado, and I usually had more copy than I had space for. I had student reporters under me and I hated to not run one of their stories, so I'd really work hard to get it to fit on the page. I'd go through it really methodically, word by word, to tighten things."

The payoff, says Couch, "was a revelation to me. The trimming away made the writing so much stronger because words that weren't necessary weren't there and the reader didn't have to wade through clutter to get to the real meaning. It's like taking a fuzzy dog to a groomer. He shaves away all the fuzz and pretty soon you start to see the shape of the real dog. All that extra fluff is hiding what you are trying to get across."

Trim Some More

It is hard to overemphasize the need for tightening during the revision process. Lisa Couch puts it this way: "I think the tightening process is the most important part of writing, and I think it's the most neglected. . . . If [writers] would take the time to go through that process and be relentless and pick out the words they don't need, rephrase to tighten, and choose the one correct word instead of the almost-correct series of words, they'd be a lot better off."

The tightening process, as we will see in later chapters, doesn't have to be a time-consuming, difficult one.

"Once you've done this kind of tightening on a lot of stories, it just gets to be part of your writing process," says Lisa Couch, "and it doesn't take that much longer to do it. But your writing is so much better. The shape of the dog comes through, if you know what I mean."

Get Focused

One of the major problems that you will run into in revising your own work is focus. The creative mind is free to wander from topic to topic in that first draft, but in the revision process your editing mind has to learn to recognize the one major theme or focus of your story, and make certain that everything in the piece, every word, works toward that theme. You will see more about this in Chapter 4.

Remembering this focus is a useful tool in trimming, as well. To see how paying attention to the story's focus can help, try writing down a few words that summarize the focus of the story at the top of your first draft. Then, as you read through the piece, ask yourself if each passage is in line with that focus.

Greg Couch recalls a story of his where focus was a major factor in his revision process.

"Probably the story I put the most effort into recently was one about a local boxer, a club fighter, who got a shot against the world champ. I drove with this boxer from Wichita to Omaha. I came back at the end of spending three or four days with him and wrote 135 or 140 inches (nearly 25 pages of manuscript) on him.

"Then, with Lisa constantly reminding me to be relentless in my cuts—I spent a week editing it—I reread it over 50 times. I read every sentence, and every phrase within every sentence to see if it drove home the point I was making in the story, and if anything did not hit it right there, then we cut it out. In the end, the revision job really made that story."

You can read the final draft of that story in Appendix A.

Discover Trouble Spots

One of the tricks veteran writers have learned is to recognize their trouble spots and focus their editing attention on those areas. Sometimes these trouble spots are quite specific, other times they are more general.

I have a "your/you're" problem. My editing mind certainly knows the difference between the two, but my writing mind just can't seem to get it right. When I have finished a story, I do a computer word search for every "you" in the story, and make sure I have handled them all correctly.

I also tend to use "of course" much too often, and go through every story I write to make sure I haven't used that phrase more than once.

Joe Bargmann's trouble spot is more general. "I use too many words," he admits. "I overwrite. Even in a single paragraph, I overwrite. When I go back and look at my first drafts I try to weed out as much as I can, but it's tough work."

Also, Bargmann admits, "When I haven't done enough reporting or when I'm tired I tend to tell more than I show, and I need to reverse that. It usually takes additional reporting and it lengthens the story, but it's important (as we will see in Chapter 5) to show the reader the details of the story, not just tell the reader the summary."

Triple-Edit Your Copy

To make sure your editing mind does a good job using some of these techniques, you may find it useful to think of revision as a three-step process that incorporates one or more of these techniques in each step.

The first step is to go through your story looking for basic problems with spelling, capitalization, grammar and usage faults (a dangling participle, for instance), and the like. This is the best place to use the techniques mentioned for line-by-line edits, such as Lisa Couch's use of a blank piece of paper under each line of copy in her story.

The second step is to go through the story again, this time looking for focus and flow problems. Ask yourself if each paragraph logically follows the one before.

A good technique here is to take that blank piece of paper and cover the paragraph that follows the one you are reading. When you get to the end of each paragraph, ask yourself (out loud, if that will help slow you down and won't bring too many odd glances your way) what comes next. Then see if the next paragraph does, indeed, provide that information.

Chapters 2, 3, and 4 contain a good deal more about this sort of editing and revision.

The third step is to revise for style, which we will discuss in Chapter 5. Not all stories lend themselves to this polishing of style, in which you may add as much material as you take away, but the stories that do can become award-winners if your editing and revision can truly bring the story alive for the reader.

Some Final Thoughts

Joe Bargmann from *Seventeen* magazine is an inveterate reviser. For him, the old saying that great stories aren't written, they are rewritten, is, as he says, "absolutely true. I firmly believe in the revision process."

Bargmann adds that for any beginning writer, or any veteran writer, for that matter, "You have to realize that your copy is malleable. Your story, your words, are your clay, and you've got to form the story out of them, and it's important to remember always that how you form the story at first is not how it's going to end up."

Bargmann says that during his years editing at *Seventeen* only one story has come across his desk and then gone into the magazine in almost exactly the same form. All the rest have been through significant revision.

As for his own writing, "I've never had a story of mine that didn't go through meaningful revision. Some writers seem afraid to say that, like it's some sort of deficiency on their part, but I think it's quite the opposite. Revision, for me, is where the story comes alive."

Exercises

1. The next time you finish a first draft of a story, do an immediate edit on it, looking for misspellings, typographical errors, grammar problems, and the like. Set the story aside for a few days. When you come back to it, read it aloud, trying to catch the same kinds of mistakes you looked for in the first edit. If you find errors—and you probably will—you will have just learned the importance of "Changing Your Mind."

2. Using one of your own stories or one from another writer, see if you can reduce its overall length by one-third. If it's a six-page story, for instance, pare it down to four pages. Then have someone read the shorter version for the first time and get his or her reaction. Most likely, the reader won't feel the piece is missing anything. What does that tell you about those two pages you edited out?

2

Revising
the Hook

As veteran writers know and beginners soon learn, one of the keys to effective revising is understanding that every story is a construction project. Whether you are writing a news story, a public relations brochure, a high-style magazine piece or any other kind of nonfiction story, there are basic story elements that serve as your building blocks for that construction. These blocks include the hook or lead of a story and the information, background, quote, description, and anecdote blocks that make up the body of the story.

How well you revise those blocks in your final draft, and then how well you connect the blocks together, will make the difference between a story that grabs and holds your readers' interest and one that does not.

As we discussed in Chapter 1, you probably won't be thinking of these blocks as you write—most writers do not. When the writing is going well you sit at your word processor and type, giving very little thought to blocks or transitions. Instead, you are focused on your reporting and how to turn that reporting into a readable story.

But once you are in the revision process you have the time and perspective to recognize the story's construction and work on making sure that each block fits with its neighbors before and behind it to form a smooth unit within the section. Then you can make sure that all the sections fit together smoothly, as well, so that the story becomes a flowing, seamless whole.

Kinds of Hooks

The hook begins your story. All of the building blocks are important and most stories you write will likely contain all or most of them, but the hook is the most important block of them all, especially for beginning writers, because it is with these first few sentences of the story that you entice the reader (or, perhaps more importantly, the editor) into starting your story.

In the newspaper business, this opening is often called the lead (sometimes spelled "lede," to avoid confusion with the hot lead that was once used in the typesetting process for daily newspapers). Most news stories in newspapers open with a tightly written, information-packed paragraph that summarizes the story's most important points. This is called a *summary lead.*

Summary leads developed in newspapers partly in response to the reader's desire for quick information and partly in response to design needs.[1] Not only does the summary lead provide a quick one- or two-sentence synopsis of the story's content, it also sets up a structure for the story (called the inverted pyramid, where the most important information is at the top of the story and the least important at the bottom), which allows the story to be cut very quickly to fit into an allotted space on the page.

Also, reader surveys show that many of today's busy readers never get past the first few paragraphs of a story before moving on to the next one, so it is crucial that the story's most important elements be presented at the start.

In magazine writing, and in some newspaper feature writing where the reader's needs are different from the frenzied quick read of breaking news stories, the story's opening is frequently called "the hook" and is thought of in different terms from the summary lead.

With a *feature hook*, the writer doesn't necessarily try to summarize the story as quickly as he or she can. Instead, a feature hook should grab the reader through techniques that combine entertainment value (in the sense of drama, tension, and the like) and news content. Three of the most common kinds of feature hooks are the descriptive, narrative, and startle hooks.

Here are examples of a summary lead and also of the three kinds of feature hooks.

> ### Summary lead:
>
> The government is ordering a recall of Japanese-made seat belts on millions of cars, minivans and sport utility vehicles sold from 1986 through 1991 because of concerns the buckles sometimes fail to latch or unlatch.[2]
>
> ### Descriptive hook:
>
> Charlie Crist could hear the inmates' voices whispering behind him, and for once, the senator who's normally a picture of composure was getting nervous.[3]
>
> ### Narrative hook:
>
> I'm kneeling down behind home plate at St. Petersburg's Al Lang Field on a perfect Sunday morning in November, waiting for our game to begin, looking out toward the dark dirt and clay of the infield, the way my father used to see it. Beyond is the green perfection of the outfield meadow.[4]
>
> ### Startle hook:
>
> Parkinson's disease breeds desperation. Relentless and incurable, Parkinson's affects as many as 1.5 million Americans, most older than 60. It slowly destroys their bodies, and, sometimes, their minds.[5]

Revising Hooks

In revising leads or hooks, you need to learn to recognize both *internal* and *external* problems and to fix those trouble spots.

Internal Problems

The major internal problem with hooks usually is the writer's inability to keep the hook or lead as tight as possible. In newspaper and magazine writing, especially, your story is often in competition with many other stories for the reader's attention. If your hook doesn't quickly capture the reader, then he or she will move onto a hook or lead that does.

This problem is solved first through a slow, careful edit of the hook to make sure that every word is necessary (for more on this kind of editing, see Chapter 7.)

Next, it is important to remember the purpose of each kind of hook and revise to make sure your hook doesn't try to do too much—this is a common failing. A summary lead, for instance, is meant only to summarize, not to provide detail. If you try to provide too much detail, the reader may feel confused by the flood of information and abandon the story before you can begin to explain things in subsequent paragraphs.

Note, for instance, in the summary lead example earlier that the writer did not mention the names of the car companies that use the seat belts in question, the models of cars or trucks involved, the manufacturer of the seat belts, or the cost of the recall. Instead, the writer summarized rather broadly, making the major point of the story—the seat-belt recall—clearly and concisely for the reader.

For the reader with time and interest in the details, they are all there in the second and third paragraphs of the story, which expand on the summary material presented in the lead. For the harried reader who only wants or needs the highlights, though, the lead gets the job done quite nicely.

Similarly, the descriptive hook should limit itself to a quick, relevant description and not explain too much of the story's detail. Note how the descriptive hook above does just that, describing one sound and its implications. The details come later in the story.

The narrative and startle hooks must likewise be limited and tightly written in order to hold the reader's interest.

Narrative hooks are often a bit longer than the other kinds of hooks, because they are describing ongoing action. Even here, however, brevity is a virtue. In the example shown, the narrative hook is limited to setting the scene—home plate at St. Petersburg's Al Lang Field—and connecting it to the story's apparent theme, the emotional ties between a father and son.

Startle hooks are usually very brief, because the hook's impact is derived, at least in part, from its punchy, quick-hit nature. A startle hook may include some detail for impact, as in the example, but those details are limited, and it comes to its point quite quickly.

In all three types of hooks, the reader is brought into the story quickly with an interesting, but brief, introduction to the story's content. (Remember again that your leads or hooks are in a competition with others.)

External Problems

The other type of problem you will encounter as you revise your hooks is external. Quite frequently you may discover during the revision process that what you once thought was a terrific hook no longer accurately reflects the story you have written.

This problem results from a disagreement between your creative mind and your editing mind. As your creative mind works on a story, the piece begins to change and to head in new directions. Even when these changes are relatively minor, they often accumulate until, by the story's end, the original hook no longer really seems to belong with the piece at all.

In the narrative hook example shown earlier, for instance, the story began as a first-person piece on men over 40 playing amateur baseball. Only during the revision process did it occur to me that much of the story was really about the connection that playing the game again in middle age made in my mind with my father, who played major league baseball in the 1950s. In the third revision the hook was changed to reflect that father-son connection.

To revise your story to handle this problem, you must first recognize what the story has become (Chapter 1 gives you some hints on how to see the story fresh so you can accomplish this) and then revise the hook to reflect the new focus.

In many cases the internal and external problems work together to weaken a hook, and a good revision will not only tighten the hook, but will also focus it more narrowly on the story that you have actually written.

For example, Sherry Long, a student writer trying for her first published story, wrote a first draft of a travel story about Edinburgh, Scotland, that included this hook:

> For centuries, Edinburgh has been at the heart of Scottish history. Pack a comfortable pair of tennis shoes, a light jacket and strong sense of adventure and you will be prepared to experience a city full of charm, history and art.

That's a decent hook for a first draft. But Long realized as she worked her way through the rest of her first draft that Edinburgh's walkability had become her theme. In her second draft, her hook became something more like this:

> Edinburgh, Scotland's capital, is a wonderful city for walking. Pack a comfortable pair of shoes, a light jacket and a strong sense of adventure to experience this city full of charm, history and art.

You can see that this revision starts right off with the walking theme in the first sentence, then takes that theme and uses it in the second sentence to bring in the ideas of charm, history, and art in Edinburgh.

By narrowing her focus in this way, Long also tightened her hook, dropping the section about "the heart of Scottish history."

In her final draft, the one that sold to a mid-size daily newspaper's Sunday travel section, the hook looked like this:

> Edinburgh, Scotland's capital, is a wonderful city for walking. All that you need to see most everything in this compact and beautiful city full of charm, history and art is a comfortable pair of shoes, a light jacket and a strong sense of adventure.

As you can see, the editors at the newspaper kept the central theme of walking in the first sentence, then turned the second sentence around to get at the elements of charm, history, and art right away, bringing the walking theme back at the end of the hook. The editors also asked Long to reinsert the qualitative statement about the city's appeal ("compact and beautiful") in the hook to add to the hook's information value.

"Every time I revised this story it changed," recalls Long. "But the more I thought about it, the more it seemed to me that walking was what the story was really focused on. So I knew I had to change the hook to reflect that emphasis, and when I did I felt that the whole story finally fell into place."

Long's story, both first draft and final, is reprinted in Appendixes B and C.

You will probably find yourself doing the same kind of revision, working on the body of the story first as you revise, and then going back to revise the hook to mesh with the body. This is a useful, logical way to work toward a well-connected final draft.

Exercises

1. Take a look at the "Scene on Bayshore" story reprinted in Appendixes H and I. What kind of hook has the writer used for this piece? Describe how the hook changed from its first draft to the published version. What did the changes accomplish?

2. How does the fourth paragraph of the final version (Appendix I) help the hook connect to the rest of the story? How does it compare to the third paragraph of the first draft (Appendix H)? Describe the function of these paragraphs in the story and analyze why the newspaper editors liked the final version better.

3. Your editor just asked you to write a summary lead for that same story. Do that and explain how the new lead affects the story. Do the same for a startle hook.

Notes

1. And partly, it is said, as a way for Civil War newspaper correspondents to make sure that the most important elements of a battlefield story got through before the telegraph lines were cut.
2. Associated Press story by Catherine O'Brien, from the *Tampa Tribune*, May 22, 1995.
3. From "Chain Gang Charlie Crist gets plenty of recognition," in the *Tampa Tribune*, May 22, 1995, by Vickie Chachere.
4. From the *Tampa Tribune*, November 1995, by Rick Wilber.
5. From "Risky Relief," in the *Tampa Tribune*, May 22, 1995, by Lindsay Peterson.

3

Revising Blocks

As you work on revising your blocks, you will need to pay as much attention to the story's other components as you do to its hook, and then smoothly connect them all together. For most nonfiction stories, these other basic blocks are information blocks, background blocks, quote blocks, description blocks, and anecdote blocks.

Information Blocks

Information blocks are those paragraphs that provide factual support and detail for your story. They are important because they prove what you are saying in the story is true and because they establish credibility for you as the writer. This is important, of course, in newspaper and magazine writing, and even more important in public relations writing, where persuasion is frequently part of the information process.

This makes information blocks vital, but it also makes them slow going for many readers, because they are likely to be filled with data. To help the readers, tighten your information blocks as much as possible by getting rid of anything that is not essential to the story. Remember, the information you are telling the reader may be important, but too much of this good thing can slow the reader down.

For instance, for her story on Attention Deficit Disorder (ADD) for *Seventeen* magazine, Jeannette Batz did an early draft that contained several paragraphs of quite specific medical information on the disorder.

Later, after working with her editor at *Seventeen*, Batz culled that information paragraph to this:

> Basically, ADD distorts the way the brain sends and receives messages. The pattern of symptoms changes with each individual. Some kids are distracted, quiet, and dream; others talk incessantly and are given to impulsive bursts of energy, anger or both.

This winnowing-down process was important to Batz as she worked on the piece. Putting an overabundance of detail into the early drafts helped her choose what to keep in later drafts.

"The first drafts of the story had several really long and complex paragraphs full of medical and psychological information," she says. "I wasn't sure how much girls of 16 or 17 would want to know, so I wrote it at the max knowing that during revision I could take out anything I thought was too much detail."

When you revise your information blocks, remember to come back to the story fresh (take a look back at Chapter 1 for some ideas on how to do that) and try deleting facts from the information blocks. Does the block still do its job with that fact missing? If so, consider deleting it.

You may discover, as Batz did, that the information you put into the first draft contained facts that supported your conclusions. As you revise, however, you may discover redundancies; that is, several different blocks contain those important facts, so some of them can be deleted.

It was, perhaps, important for you to find the information and important to write it into the first draft, because it seemed that later material would depend on these facts. Once you realize that the conclusions don't depend solely on those facts, however, you can get rid of the unneeded material. One or two bits of data may be plenty to support your point. You do not have to use all of the supportive facts available to you. In fact, if you have ten or twelve facts and can pick the best few to use in the story, that helps ensure their effectiveness.

Make sure that every information paragraph and everything *in* every information paragraph is absolutely necessary for the reader to know.

Sometimes, of course, you will want the information to be very specific. At other times you will want to keep the information minimal. The decision is yours and your editor's, and is based on your knowledge of who your readers are.

It is a good idea to save all of your deleted material. This is easy to do if you are using a computer. Start another file in your software package where you can keep the deleted material, then just move it from the story into that file and save it there. Remember that the item you deleted in the second draft of the story may become something you want back in the third draft.

Background Blocks

Closely related to information blocks are background blocks, those paragraphs or sentences that give your story a sense of its place in history, or a context. This can be crucial in the reader's appreciating the importance of some element of the story, or for seeing how one element fits logically with another.

In a story that freelance writer Jennifer Wittwer wrote on champion speed water-skier Corey Cook, for instance, the two-paragraph background block went like this:

> During his off-season in the U.S., Cook visits other countries, such as Australia, to observe their ski racers and compete. For eight years, he has raced in some of the largest tournaments in Australia, winning a number of them. He is two-time Australian International Champion and the New South Wales Men's State Champion. He says he enjoys racing Australia's tough competitors and challenging courses because it keeps him in shape for the U.S. season.
>
> Some of Cook's most outstanding accomplishments include: four-time U.S. Men's National Champion; six-time U.S. High-Point Champion, and two-time Alcatraz–San

Francisco Bay Challenge winner (he is current record holder for this race). At age 14, Cook set the Junior Boys time record for the Catalina Ski Race in 1987, and his record still stands.

The revision process for background blocks is similar to that for information blocks, in that both kinds of blocks need to be as tight as possible. Compare the first draft and final draft of the Cook story, reprinted in Appendixes D and E, to see how Wittwer and the editors at *The Water Skier* magazine revised this block.

Background blocks are often a lot more interesting to read than information blocks. As the Cook piece illustrates, a background block may well be entertaining and informative in its own right, as well as an important context-setter for your story.

For instance, say you are writing a personality piece on a local business leader who is retiring. A background paragraph on him might look something like this:

During the last part of the War in the Pacific, Smith was a flight engineer and top turret gunner on a B-25 that flew regular bombing missions over mainland Japan. On August 6, 1945, he was in his turret, swiveling the guns to make sure they moved freely, when there was a bright flash of light and then a huge mushroom cloud began to grow on the horizon. Smith and his crewmates thought it must have been a firestorm from an incendiary raid. It was, instead, the atom bomb that another plane, *Enola Gay*, had dropped that morning on Hiroshima.

You can see that the background block adds measurably to the reader's understanding of the businessman and his life. The block has its own interest value, as well, and so serves a dual purpose.

Like information blocks, background blocks vary from broad, accessible background to quite specific background depending on the audience.

In Jeannette Batz's story for *Seventeen*, the background came in paragraphs like this:

Until now, guys have been diagnosed with ADD at a much higher rate than girls. This is mainly because hyperactivity is the most common—and obvious—tip-off that someone might have ADD, and guys tend to be a lot more hyper than girls. But now doctors think that ADD may be much more common among girls than previously believed.

Batz's original version had more specific information on ADD rates in males and females, but her editor took out the details to make the story more accessible to his readers.

In revising, it is important to remember that background paragraphs, like information paragraphs, can almost always be tightened, and need to be strictly relevant to the story. Remember, though, that background blocks usually hold reader interest more easily than information blocks, and so can often go longer and contain more specific detail.

Quote Blocks

Quote blocks are important to your story because they establish a line of communication directly between the reader and the person being quoted. Your job, as the intermediary or bridge between the speaker and the reader, is first of all to be fair and accurate both in the quotes you choose to use and in the way you use them (you can see more about this in Chapter 10). In terms of story structure, though, your job with quotes is to use them effectively to move the story along. Beginning writers sometimes do little more with a quote than repeat the material that introduced it. For instance, take a look at the following:

> Jones has been the coach at Tyrone High for 30 years, and watched the school go from a rural institution of some 500 hundred students to a sprawling suburban campus of nearly 4,000.
> "Since I've been here," Jones said, "Tyrone has grown immensely. We've gone from being quite rural and small to being a really large campus."

You can see how the quote merely repeats the introductory thought, and so it accomplishes little in the story. A better quote block might have gone like this:

> "I can remember when there were cows grazing on our football practice field," said Jones. "Back then we were lucky

to get a couple of dozen kids to come out for the team, and the first thing we had them do was shoo the cows off the field."

Instead of repeating information already found in the story, the quote should take that information and do something productive with it—expand the information and provide color or personal detail that helps make the information real for the reader, adding a human touch to otherwise dry information.

See how Jeannette Batz did this in her story on Attention Deficit Disorder:

This stubbornness, too, can be softened by Ritalin. Stacy Conant, a 13-year-old with ADD from Bellevue, Washington, says, "It makes me happy, more willing to do things. If I wasn't taking it, someone would ask me, 'Would you do this for me?'—just a simple little thing—and I'd go, 'No!' When I'm taking it, I say, 'Sure!' "

You can see how the quote from the 13-year-old amplifies and provides a personal look at the brief introductory statement about how stubbornness can be softened.

At their best, quotes can not only provide personal detail, but even provide the information on which the detail is focused. In that same story, Batz has the following quote block:

After living with ADD for eight years, 16-year-old Jennifer Creasy, a preacher's daughter from Bedford, Virginia, can tell when it's making her "kind of obnoxious. I'm really hyper, out of control. If my mom asks me to do something, I'll complain a lot and won't do it right away, and she'll have to ask me a few times, because I don't listen."

In this case, the beginning of the actual quote offers the information (that ADD makes her "kind of obnoxious") and the remainder of the quote offers the personal details. That is effective writing, because it is tight, informative, and keeps the story moving along.

As you revise quote blocks, then, make sure each quote is internally as tight as it can be, avoiding redundancies and wordy expressions, and that each quote does something useful for the story, either expanding information just offered or offering something new and relevant by itself.

A good way to do this is to isolate each quote block in the story and run through this list of questions:

1. Can I tighten this quote to make it more effective?
2. Does this quote illuminate the information offered in the previous sentence or two?
3. Does this quote offer a personal glimpse?
4. Does this quote give the story more human interest?

If it doesn't do one or more of those things, either pull the quote from the story as you revise, or replace it with one that does do some of those things.

Remember that with quote blocks, as with the other blocks we talk about in this chapter, your reporting comes first. If you don't have other, better quotes to use in the place of the one you have discovered is weak, then you have limited your options in terms of revising the story.

Description Blocks

There are several things to consider as you go through your story revising your description blocks. One of them is that description blocks are more effective when the description is detailed and specific. It is better to note that an infielder on a baseball team is using a Rawlings model XPG6H glove than to simply say he wears a mitt. It is an accumulation of these specific items that make something real for the reader, rather than a general blur.

Using the baseball example, a beginning writer might say that a player steps up to the plate and gets ready to hit. A more polished writer might put it this way:

> The pine tar sticks to his hand as he steps into the box. The bat, a Louisville Slugger, feels good, the handle slim, the weight out at the barrel. He takes a swing or two to loosen up, feels the shoulders rotate through, the right wrist roll over the left at the end of the swing.
>
> He digs a small hole for his right foot in the dirt of the batter's box, a place he can push from as he swings, and

then, as the pitcher stares in for the sign, he bends a bit at
the knees, brings the bat back toward his right shoulder, and
stares out toward the mound, and waits.

Note how the specific details add to this description block
by making the scene more vivid than would a general, simple
statement that the batter came to the plate and waited for the
pitch.

Like the other blocks discussed in this chapter, the description block can be overdone. Too much detail can swamp the
reader and make for confusion, not clarity.

When you are revising your description blocks you will most
often be trimming them. Rarely these days does a writer have
the space in a newspaper, magazine, or public relations piece
to use all the detail that he or she would like, so you need to
sharpen the detail inside each descriptive block and also cull
out those blocks that are not fully useful to your story. In the
passage above, for instance, you can see how the second
paragraph alone would suffice with a few minor edits if space
was tight in the publication.

Occasionally, though, you will see as you revise that *more*
detail would help the piece, if you have the space. Try replac-
ing some general statement with a more specific one. For
example, "They walked past several tall trees," could become
"They walked past two large grandfather oaks and several
sycamores." See if it helps make the story more accurate and
more fun to read.

It is worth remembering that description refers to more
than just sight. The other senses are effective, too, in adding
detail. Note how the paragraphs about the baseball player add
significant elements of touch to the block. Elements of sound,
taste, and smell could just have effectively been part of the
block, too, though you will be wise to try to keep any one block
to one or two of the senses to avoid reader confusion.

Finally, as you must do with the other blocks, make sure
your descriptive blocks are relevant to the story. It would be
easy to fall into a long block describing in loving detail the kind
of automobile the batter drives, but unless that adds something important to the story (in some circumstances, it might)
it is probably better left out in favor of details of his appearance at the plate.

During the revision process you can also ask yourself if other senses than sight could reasonably work in this spot.

Here again it is critical that you have done a solid job of reporting first, before you begin revising your description. Otherwise, when you realize that you could add details such as weather or the sound of the crowd, you won't have that material in your notes and you will have to do more reporting to acquire it. That can be a time-consuming and occasionally expensive process, and sometimes is not possible at all.

Anecdote Blocks

Anecdotes are those little stories within your story that help make it real and keep it interesting for the reader. Anecdotes give a story life by bringing real people into it and connecting them to otherwise dry information or unattached description.

Some of the other blocks discussed in this chapter can also be anecdotal. Certainly a narrative hook is anecdotal, and a descriptive hook might be, as well. Background blocks are frequently anecdotal, in that they tell a story while giving background. The example earlier in this chapter of the WW II flight engineer is a good example of a background anecdote.

Quote blocks, too, can be anecdotal when the subject of a magazine piece, for example, relates an interesting story. The major problem that you will find with your anecdotes when revising is relevancy. Sometimes, you may have what you think is a great anecdote, and try your best to force it into the story. If the anecdote doesn't belong there, this forced effort will be all too obvious.

In revising, identify and isolate the anecdote, and then ask yourself if it really connects to the story at hand. For example, see how this quote block anecdote from Jeannette Batz's ADD story makes a firm connection to her story's theme:

> ADD doesn't show up the same way in all girls. It makes Christy spacey and distracted; people used to call her a "dizzy blond," a "space cadet." She remembers one day in particular: "In third grade, my favorite teacher told me I was blaming my problems on everybody else when they were really all my fault. I burst into tears . . . It's *always* been hard for me to pay attention."

You can see how Christy's quote about herself brings her problem to life, makes it real for the reader, and directly pertains to the topic of ADD and young girls. (By the way, you may have noticed that this is also a background block.) A similar story about Christy's past that was equally interesting (perhaps something about her first date, or a trip) but not directly tied to ADD would not work as well in this story.

Just as with the other blocks, as you revise your anecdotes keep them as tight as you can, but also include specific facts and details. As you have done with the other blocks, the best way to go about this revision process is to identify and isolate the anecdotes, then tighten them up as much as you can. Once you have done that, ask yourself if they really help the story by making your subject more interesting, more human, for the reader. Then, finally, make sure they absolutely fit into your story's theme and purpose.

If your anecdote is not both interesting and relevant, you might consider dropping it in favor of one that is. If you have done a good job of reporting, you will have others to choose from.

Here is a handy checklist for revising all the blocks in your story:

Checklist for Blocks

1. **Make them tight.** Make sure the information blocks contain only the necessary information, depending on your audience and your editor.

2. **Make them relevant.** Make sure the blocks are relevant, as well as interesting.

3. **Save your changes.** Start a new file for all the phrases, sentences, or paragraphs of information that you delete from a story in your first revision of it. These changes might return in the next draft, and by saving your deletions you avoid having to reconstruct them from your notes.

4. **Do your reporting first.** If you have not done sufficient research, you will not have much of an information block. You need a lot of information to support a story, and the only way to get that is through reporting.

As a general rule of thumb, if you use more than half your research for information blocks in your story, you didn't do enough reporting.

Exercises

1. Go through Jeannette Batz's story on attention deficit disorder (reprinted in Appendix G) and define each block in the story. How many information blocks are there? How many background blocks? Quote blocks? Description blocks? Anecdote blocks? What do these numbers tell you about the focus of the story? If the story had been a personality piece on just one of the young girls mentioned, which kind of block might have dominated? Why?

2. Go through the final version of D. Quentin Wilber's "Scene on Bayshore" story (reprinted in Appendix I) and identify its blocks. In this story's description blocks, identify the specific details that help make these blocks successful. Are there any blocks you might rewrite to increase their effectiveness?

3. Which blocks in Wilber's first draft of the "Scene on Bayshore" story (Appendix H) were dropped in the final draft? Why? Which ones were added? Why?

4. In Jennifer Wittwer's story on water-skier Corey Cook, which quote blocks were added to the final draft (Appendix E)? Why do you think editor Jonathan Cullimore wanted these quotes in the story?

4

Arranging
Your Story

Like most newspaper writers, *Wichita Eagle* sportswriter Greg
Couch regularly writes to meet a deadline. He is a heavy
reviser, though, even when he faces that daily pressure. Couch's
typical technique is to revise as he goes, sentence by sentence,
and then, when he gets to the end of the story, he says, "I go
back and do it all once again, and then once again after that,
in its entirety, trying to get it right."

What Couch searches for in those final revisions is the best
arrangement of the story; that is, the best possible way to fit
the various blocks together to tell his story. Do the same thing
as you revise, asking yourself the following three questions:

1. Does one block follow the previous one logically?
2. Are there smooth transitions between the blocks so
   the reader is carried effortlessly along?
3. Are there places where the blocks can be trimmed
   or even deleted, so that the story moves faster for
   the reader?

To answer the first question, about logical progression, try
isolating the blocks and thinking of them as pieces of a puzzle.
If you put these pieces in the right place, you will have a

successful story. If just one or two are out of place, though, the puzzle doesn't fit together the way it should and your story is less successful. In many cases, if the blocks don't logically follow, your reader may feel that things don't quite make sense in the story.

So, the first thing you need to think about as you look at your first draft and think about how to improve it is whether or not you have presented your material in the right order.

Arranging Blocks and Sections

In longer stories, it is very common to gather a number of related blocks into what we will call a *section*. Each section is composed of several or many blocks working together to present an anecdote or scene or to present information. These sections are often broken up by subheads (a common technique in newspaper writing) or by one- or two-line space breaks (commonly found in magazine writing).

In a shorter story for a newspaper or magazine, the entire story may be, in effect, one section. In that case, all you have to do is rearrange the blocks so that they form the best possible story, as we will see later in this chapter.

First Section

In a lengthier piece, the lead section of a story is usually composed of a one- or two-paragraph hook, followed by a background block and perhaps an information block or a quote. See, for instance, the following opening section from Couch's story about a local Wichita boxer who was given a chance to fight against a world champion:

> The bleeding finally stops, and Steve Langley waits behind half a dozen boxers lined up at the cashier's chain-link window to collect their pay. Fifteen minutes earlier he was leaning backward over a dirty sink in a dirty bathroom while three stitches were hurriedly sewn into his forehead to stop the blood that had been spurting straight up as if from a sprinkler.

The blood had stopped the fight 1½ minutes into the second round, when Langley and world welterweight champion Maurice Blocker simultaneously threw jabs and accidentally butted heads on the follow-through.

Although Langley had landed the only two solid punches, under the rules, the fight hadn't gone enough rounds for the judges to determine a winner. The ruling: technical draw.

"A draw? With the world champion?" the other boxers in line say to Langley. "People fight a lifetime for something like that. With a world champion? Twenty years from now you'll be telling people. You had a draw? With a. . . ."

It does serve as consolation. After all, how often does a machine worker from a Wichita plastics plant get a chance to fight a world champ? Much less fight him to a draw?

But Langley sees only a lost chance to prove himself.

And then, another blow, out of the ring, the kind that hurts Langley more in the hours and days after the fight than any of Blocker's punches.

As he's handed his pay, an amount he isn't willing to disclose—"and don't forget the 200 for expenses"—Langley's hit with the news that the decision has been changed after complaints from the champ's corner.

The new ruling: no contest. As if the whole thing never happened.

Before the fight, he had said that a guy like him would never get a shake against a champ.

Then the stomach churned. And the pressure grew. And the bell sounded. And the biggest fight in Steve Langley's life never happened.

"If this never happened," he says afterward, "I must not be here."

You can see how Couch opens with a narrative hook of the boxer waiting in line. He follows that with a background block, and then a quote. The quote is followed with more background (about Langley's job as a machine worker), and then another information block on the changed fight ruling. Finally, the section ends with another background block and the final quote.

All of this material together comprises the opening section of the story. If you look at Appendix A, which includes a reprint of the entire story, you can see how a space break after the "I must not be here" quote clearly ends the opening section, stopping the story's flow momentarily and preparing the reader for a change in the writer's technique. In this particular instance, the change is one of time sequence.

There are two important questions to consider as you revise sections. First, does the order of the blocks within the section work successfully, or should the order be changed? Second, is the entire section in the right place, or should it be moved?

In other words, *placement* is the key to revising sections and the blocks within sections.

As you can see when you read Couch's entire story, the basic structure for his story is chronological.

Couch follows the boxer from early Wednesday morning through the abortive Thursday night fight and then the long drive home early Friday morning.

The opening section clearly comes from toward the end of the chronology, yet Couch has used it to begin the story. Why?

"Well," he explains, "I was going to write this piece with a straight chronology, but I realized after I'd gotten into it that this story is really about respect, and how Langley couldn't get any respect at all. I thought he stood for all club fighters in that sense. And that opening scene, for me, really showed the lack of respect he was getting."

So Couch pulled out the section from near the end, put it up front, then turned to his straight chronological scheme with his second section.

The result is a powerful hook that brings the reader into the story with a sympathetic narrative of the boxer and some background information, and also serves to establish the story's theme of a lack of respect for Langley.

As you saw in Chapter 2, writers often bury their hooks when writing the first draft of a story. During revisions, you may well discover that your best hook is found somewhere in the middle or toward the end of your first draft.

When you find the hook there, you should move it to the beginning and then blend it smoothly into the body of the story as Couch did with his story. The trick, of course, is finding the buried hook. Here are two hints on how to find a buried hook:

1. Ask yourself what the theme of your story is. For more on theme, see Chapter 5. Identify the theme and then find the section or sections that you think best discuss the theme.
2. Ask yourself what moment or moments in your story have the most emotional impact or are the most important items for the reader to know. Identify the section or sections that contain that moment. There should be just one or two if your story is as tightly focused as you would like it to be.

Now, see if the section or sections that you have identified from the two questions above are the same. Because the emotional highpoints of a story usually set the theme, it is quite likely that the sections *are* the same. If that is the case, try moving that section to the beginning of your story and see how it works.

If the sections are different for questions one and two, try moving the section that contains the emotional highpoint or most important information to the beginning of the story, and see how that works. If it seems to work effectively, you may have misidentified the theme. In that case, ask yourself a few questions about the theme. If you are confident that your theme is solid, then an emotional highpoint that does not reflect that theme is not going to work in the story, at least not in the all-important beginning. So try your next-best section in terms of emotional impact and see how that works.

This process sounds more complicated and time-consuming than it really is. Put this into practice during the revision process and you will find that identifying the hook becomes easy.

Subsequent Sections

When you were writing your first draft you had to construct a technique for moving the reader through the story. Typically, that method is one of the following: declining interest or value; chronological; spatial; or otherwise organized by some sensible listing technique.

By *declining interest or value*, we mean the classic newspaper format in which you place the most important section at the top, and follow it with sections of decreasing importance as you write. This structure has worked well for the newspaper business for nearly two centuries and has its uses for the modern reader because it not only quickly gives a heavy dose of information to the busy newspaper reader, it also allows editors to easily cut the story to fit available space on the page. Because the least important information is at the bottom, editors on deadline who are working on these kinds of stories can safely cut from the bottom and still expect the story to make sense for the reader. You can find this kind of story in Section A of your daily newspaper every day.

By *chronological*, we mean that each section logically follows the previous section in time. If your second section takes place in the morning, then your third should take place sometime after that, for instance, and the fourth sometime after the third and so on. This technique is especially common for many types of newspaper feature stories and for many types of magazine articles, including personality pieces and travel stories.

The Couch piece on boxer Steve Langley is ordered chronologically.

By *spatial*, we mean that each section logically follows the previous section in terms of the space it occupies. For instance, a story might be about Las Vegas, and a logical flow would move from casino to casino down the city's main street. Or a story might be about endangered sea turtles, and the logical flow begin with a description of the beach where the turtles lay their eggs and then continue with the movement of the turtle hatchlings once the eggs hatch. The possibilities are endless, with spatial flow primarily focused on your ability to describe people or things in a logical pattern.

By *sensible listing technique* we mean that every story has some logical pattern to it, something that reasonably takes the reader through it.

Public relations writer and editor Lynne McChristian, for instance, needed to construct an informational brochure about her company, USAA Property and Casualty Insurance. After quite a bit of revision, she decided on a technique that included a welcoming message from the regional vice president, then a brief history section that established a context for the reader, then informational sections on the company's facilities and the people who work there.

"I knew the welcome had to come first," McChristian says, "but I moved the other elements around a lot as I revised. Then I decided that the history section would give the reader the background to better understand the other sections."

As a result of her revisions, the logic of McChristian's brochure is solid, one element clearly setting up the next. You can read the brochure in Appendix F.

One of the primary things that can go wrong in a story is that this logical flow of the story can fall apart somewhere. This is especially true for longer pieces, where you are trying to hold the reader's interest for a relatively long time, and trying to build to an ending that logically emerges from the body of the story.

First, look at the sections of your first draft and see what the pattern is. Is it chronological, like Greg Couch's story? Is it spatial? Does it follow a list of names or places?

Second, identify any sections that don't follow that pattern. Remember that the first section sometimes stands alone, and that the second section is frequently where the pattern is established in longer stories.

See if you can move any sections that don't follow the pattern to another place in the story where they make a better fit.

For instance, in Couch's story, the section about telling war stories could reasonably have been placed anywhere as anecdotal background information. By placing it as the fourth section, and introducing the section with a transitional sentence that establishes the time sequence ("The sweat is still dripping. . . ." tied neatly into the previous section's discussion of Langley's weight and how he must sweat to lose a few more pounds before the fight starts) Couch puts it perfectly into place chronologically.

Not only does this blend the anecdotes smoothly into the story, it also keeps the time sequence moving along for the reader. As a result, the story's flow remains uninterrupted by what is essentially a flashback, something that might otherwise disrupt the forward movement of the story by taking the reader backward, instead of forward, in time.

If a section seems out of place, try moving it. You will frequently only need to rewrite a sentence or two (at the start of the section, and sometimes at the end of the previous section) to make it fit elsewhere in the story.

Then, look within each section at the blocks and go through the same process. See if you can move them around to produce a better flow.

One final note on placement. If you are having trouble seeing the problems in logic between one block and the next or one section and the next, try this:

Take a piece of paper and place it beneath one of your blocks, as if that block were as far as you had gone in reading the story. Then ask yourself what comes next. Remember this block from Greg Couch's story?:

> The blood had stopped the fight 1½ minutes into the second round, when Langley and world welterweight champion Maurice Blocker simultaneously threw jabs and accidentally butted heads on the follow-through. Although Langley had landed the only two solid punches, under the rules, the fight hadn't gone enough rounds for the judges to determine a winner. The ruling: technical draw.

Without looking at the next block, what seems most likely to come next? Perhaps some background on exactly what a draw is in boxing. Or perhaps there will be a quote from Blocker or Langley. Or perhaps there will be an information block from Couch about the implications of that draw. But whatever comes next, it seems obvious that it will be a block that has something to do with the technical draw. Couch in fact follows the paragraph with several quotes from other boxers about the implications of the draw. (See the reprint in Appendix A.)

By blocking out the subsequent material in your first draft and simply asking yourself (in your editing frame of mind, remember) what would logically come next, you take a major step toward doing a good, solid job of revising your work.

Developing Transitions

Once you have the order of your blocks and sections revised, and you are comfortable that they logically follow one after the other, you look at your *transitions*, the words, sentences, or short paragraphs that carry the reader from each block or section to the next.

These transitions are important to your story, because they move the reader smoothly from one block or section to the next without disrupting the flow of the story. Transitions are often added in during the revision stage after you have done a lot of tinkering with the order of your blocks and sections. As the whole purpose of a transition is to keep the reader moving smoothly through the story, it is important that:

1. Transitions should not call attention to themselves. A good transition is invisible to the reader.
2. Transitions should be as brief as possible.
3. Transitions should make clear the connection between blocks or sections, leaving no doubts in the reader's mind that the flow is logical.

Among the best kinds of transitions are the single word transitions, frequently the *conjunctive adverbs.* A list of conjunctive adverbs is a useful tool for a writer to have. Some of the more common conjunctive adverbs are *accordingly, although, at the same time, besides, consequently, for example, furthermore, however, in addition, instead, meanwhile, namely, nevertheless, on the other hand, second (third, fourth . . .), still, therefore, thus.*

Another useful group of words for transition purposes are the *correlative conjunctions.* Some of the more typical correlative conjunctions are *as . . . as, both . . . and, either . . . or, neither . . . nor, not only . . . but also, whether . . . or.*

Coordinating conjunctions are also useful, including the words *and* and *but.* These also serve as good transitional words, connecting or comparing equal words, phrases, or clauses.

Smart writers learn to begin their transition toward the end of one paragraph, and then follow smoothly through at the start of the next. This avoids the clumsiness that can come from transitional paragraphs (usually one sentence long) that are often redundant and almost always useful only for the transition itself.

Remember, everything in the story's structure should be aimed toward the story's thematic purpose, whatever it is you are trying to say. A clumsy transition, in calling attention to itself, detracts from that purpose.

A transition like the middle paragraph below, for instance, glares at the reader:

> Having ADD means needing to be constantly aware of how it affects you, so it helps to have a few good friends to keep you in check. "If I'm in class with a friend who knows about my ADD, and I start spacing out, she'll just kick my desk or something to wake me up," Christy says with a laugh.
>
> That's fine for when it's your friends, but it isn't always that easy to get everyone else to understand. Several of the people interviewed for this story said that teachers, especially, can be hard to convince.
>
> Jennifer says one of her fifth grade teachers decided that she "was just a discipline case. My mom went to her and explained. Once the teacher found out, she treated me a lot differently because she knew I couldn't help it."

The clumsy middle paragraph in the example above does, indeed, make the transition from having friends help to educating teachers about the problem. Notice, however, how deleting that paragraph and inserting the word "but," in the middle of the transitional sentence moves the reader more smoothly from one thought to the next and tightens the writing considerably in the process.

> Having ADD means needing to be constantly aware of how it affects you, so it helps to have a few good friends to keep you in check. "If I'm in class with a friend who knows about my ADD, and I start spacing out, she'll just kick my desk or something to wake me up," Christy says with a laugh.
>
> *Getting your friends to understand is fairly easy, but teachers can be a little harder to educate.* Jennifer says one of her fifth grade teachers decided that she "was just a discipline case. My mom went to her and explained. Once the teacher found out, she treated me a lot differently because she knew I couldn't help it."

Now, without the transitional paragraph, the story moves much more smoothly from the first idea (the help of friends) to the second idea (letting your teacher know about ADD). The word "but" that follows the comma in the first sentence of the second paragraph announces quickly and quietly to the reader that a comparison is taking place between the two ideas, and eliminates the need for the transitional paragraph.

To effectively make transitions, then, during your revision process you should try to begin the transition at the end of the previous element and lead smoothly into the next element with just a word or two.

Exercises

1. Go through Jeannette Batz's ADD story (reprinted in Appendix G), and identify the transitions. What transitional technique does Batz use most often to move from one block to the next?

2. What organizing method does Batz use to move the reader through the story? Is it declining interest or value? Chronological? Spatial? Some other listing technique? Describe how the story might have been written in a chronological or spatial fashion.

3. What method does D. Quentin Wilber use to move readers through his "Scene of Bayshore" story (Appendix I)? What transitions does the writer use to connect the various blocks? Describe how those transitions also contribute to the method used to move readers through the story.

5

The Next Level: Style

Once you have learned the basics of revising the construction of your story, you are ready for the next step, revising to achieve literary excellence in your writing.

This sort of writing is not for everyone, and not for every story, either. In many cases, however, paying attention to matters such as voice and tone, description, comparisons, pacing and texture, theme and subtext, and the like can make the difference between writing ordinary stories and writing really outstanding ones.

A wonderful anecdote about how this next level of writing can emerge comes from Herman Melville's *Moby Dick*. As Charles Child Walcutt says in his introductory notes to a Bantam Books edition of the novel, Melville was known in his day as a popular author of South Seas adventures, and when he first submitted a manuscript of the book to an English publisher he called it, "A romance of adventure, founded upon certain wild legends in the Southern Sperm Whale Fisheries, and illustrated by the author's own personal experience of two years and more as a harpooner." In other words, a straightforward sea yarn.

As a simple seagoing adventure, *Moby Dick* might have been a fun, if forgettable, book to read. Melville, though, became involved in long conversations with his friend Nathaniel Hawthorne, who saw great potential in this little sea yarn and urged Melville to revise it.

A year later, when Melville turned in the revised version of *Moby Dick*, what he had created through the hard work of editing and revision was one of the great works of English literature, a book rich and enjoyable in both its literary and its entertainment values.

Maybe you won't write *Moby Dick*. It is likely that you don't even *want* to write something of that nature.

But if you revise some of your newspaper, magazine, or public relations stories by using the techniques talked about in this chapter, you will make your copy more powerful for the reader, more emotional, more effective in its communication. All it takes is an awareness of some writing techniques and a willingness to bring them into the story where they are appropriate.

Let's define some terms, and then discuss how you can use these techniques for effective revisions.

Voice and Tone

Voice and *tone* are related terms that refer to *who* is telling the story (voice) and *how* that person is doing the storytelling (tone).

Voice is who the reader hears talking in the story, and comes from your word choice, word order, sentence length and complexity, and other similar elements of your writing. The voice in a story can be institutional, that is, the story can sound as though it is from the publication (this is the voice in which most newspaper stories are written), or the voice in a story can be very personal, very distinctively yours.

Compare the voice from the following two excerpts:

> Newly declassified Soviet Union documents detail how the KGB set up spying and subversion operations in the United States during World War II, even after promising its allies it would concentrate on the battle against Adolf Hitler.

Bugs Bunny had to work hard to win over our little pirate. Samantha, at 4 years old, was more than a little worried about having this 6-foot-tall rabbit and his assistant tuck her into bed aboard the cruise ship *Oceanic*.

You can see that first selection sounds like the voice of the newspaper talking, and it is a neutral, rather distant voice. This is appropriate for most newspaper articles, where the writer's personality is usually something to avoid.

Personal columns and many feature stories are exceptions to this in the newspaper business. On the other hand, in the magazine business, in particular, a distinctive voice is often sought out and encouraged. You can see how personal the tone is in the second example, from a travel story for a Sunday newspaper travel section that would also work well in a travel magazine.

Tone is that part of voice that displays your emotional background as you write and revise. Tone can be simple, complex, instructional, satiric, humorous, sad, happy, or any one of many more.

The most important thing to remember as you revise your story for voice and tone is to *be consistent.*

It is important to most stories that they have one voice throughout and that the tone of the voice be consistent. Any variations in voice and tone are confusing for the reader, who begins to lose track of just who is telling the story, and how that story is being told. A story that waffles between a serious persuasive tone and a sarcastic tone, for instance, may fail as a story because the reader can't keep track of which parts are meant to be taken seriously and which parts are sarcasm. In the sarcastic parts the writer's actual meaning may be the opposite of what the words say, and if the reader doesn't understand that the tone is sarcastic, the ability of the story to communicate is lost.

For instance, you can see in the following two examples that sarcasm can be confusing unless you make clear in your introduction to quotes that sarcasm is intended.

Jamison said, "Sure, I absolutely love this new plan. It will do wonders for our company."

Jamison, upset by the proposal, said sarcastically, "Sure, I absolutely love this new plan. It will do wonders for our company."

Description

One of the more important elements to stylish writing, and one that is frequently not handled well in the writer's first draft, is description.

Not all stories lend themselves to a lot of description. But in those that do there are two frequent problems in first draft stories. One is a *lack of specific detail* in description. Writers too frequently use general description when specific details would work far more effectively. The second is *inappropriate description,* where writers use specific descriptive details, but details that are not usefully relevant to the story.

Here is an example of a general description in a travel story on a family cruise to the Bahamas.

> For the four adults, the snorkeling trip was a surprising gem. Choppy water at the usual site forced the dive boat to find a different, less-frequented reef, where the coral was beautiful and there were hundreds of tropical fish covering the coral in clouds of bright colors.

That's not bad, and gives you a general feeling for what it is like to go snorkeling. But compare it to this passage from a revised version of the same story.

> The water was too choppy that day for the normal shallow-water dive, so the boat took the thirty or so snorkelers to a reef protected from the wind and waves, but much deeper in some spots than most coral reefs we've snorkeled over the years.
>
> There were a few shallow areas that the beginners seemed to enjoy, but those of us with more experience with the snorkel, fins and mask quickly found places forty or fifty feet deep where huge brain and starlet coral hugged the sandy bottom below a steep reef wall that rose toward the surface. The clarity was absolutely Bahamian, and the fish included varieties of parrotfish and angelfish along with what seemed like dozens of other types and one very large, and curious, barracuda.

You can see that using specific detail makes the passage more vivid for the reader. Importantly, it also helps establish reader trust in the writer. The reader senses that the writer is to be trusted, because the use of specific names and colors for the fish and coral indicates clearly that the writer has done his or her research.

The other thing to make sure of in your revision is that the descriptive details are relevant for that particular story. The description of the coral and tropical fish fits right into a story about a cruise, while a similar passage about gambling casinos in Nassau might have been interesting, but less relevant to a story about a family cruise.

Comparisons

Three kinds of comparisons that you may find useful in your writing are metaphors, similes, and analogies.

Metaphors are compact comparisons meant to help the reader understand something he or she has not encountered before or to understand something in a new way. For instance, Homer's classic metaphor, "the wine-dark sea," shows us the color of the Aegean, which we don't know, by comparing it to a red wine, which we know.

Similes are compact comparisons that use the words *like* or *as* in the comparison. Changing Homer's words to "The color of the sea was like dark wine" creates a simile.

Analogies are extended comparisons that are meant to illuminate something for the reader by comparing it to something the reader already knows. For instance, Homer might have spent several lines of his poem talking about dark wine, and then compared it to the color of the Aegean.

These various forms of comparison work well for the writer because they help the reader to visualize (or hear, or smell, or taste, or touch) something that he or she is not familiar with. Sometimes, the comparison may help the reader see a *familiar* situation or concept in a new, entertaining, and informative way.

One of the things you should watch out for is the mixed metaphor, in which you combine two noncompatible comparisons in one metaphor. A political columnist might say, for instance, "The president stepped up to the plate and threw a touchdown pass last night in his State of the Union address."

The idea of a baseball hitter ("stepped up to the plate") suddenly turning into a football quarterback ("threw a touchdown pass") not only confuses the reader, it may spark an unwanted laugh and cause the reader to wonder if the writer can be trusted.

Pacing

Pacing is the element of your writing that determines how quickly the reader gets through your story. Pacing comes about from such things as your choice of words, the order in which you put those words, and the amount of structural complexity in your sentences and paragraphs. It is important that your pacing be appropriate to the story and for the publication where it will be printed.

Pacing is a function of the words you choose and the length of your sentences and paragraphs. Simple one- or two-syllable words in short, subject-verb-object sentences that are, in turn, part of short, punchy paragraphs all will contribute to a fast-paced story, as in the following example.

> The man took a deep breath, smiled at them, then brought his left hand out for them to see.
>
> In it was a long knife, and while the kids watched in horror, the man began walking toward them, his eyes glazed over as if he were in a trance.
>
> Step after stumbling step he advanced right toward them.
>
> The kids, eyes wide, could only watch.

You can see that breaking this passage up into three paragraphs, keeping most of the sentences short and all the words to two syllables or fewer, and keeping the voice active all contribute to a fast pace.

On the other hand, if you use many words of three or more syllables and string them together into sentences with several phrases or clauses that are part of page-long paragraphs, your story's pace will be slower and more deliberate, because the reader must slow down to understand the material you have presented. A brief example from public relations:

There are a great number of inconsistencies in the projections as you display them. I wonder if a more proactive management stance vis-a-vis the long-range instabilities that you foresee might not alleviate some of the more chaotic elements you are predicting, and so bring the secondary predictive elements more in line with the primary and tertiary elements.

Whew. That sort of pace is appropriate for some publications, but it is slow and deliberate and requires considerable attention on the part of the reader. Unless this slow pace is clearly demanded by your editor, it is best to avoid it.

Active and Passive Voice

Active voice sentences are those in which your subject, verb, and object follow directly along behind each other, like this:

The car rounded the corner at high speed.

Passive voice sentences turn the order around, placing the object first and the subject last, like this:

The corner was rounded at high speed by the car.

Passive voice can be a problem because it slows the reader down, forcing the reader to convert the passive voice into active voice before understanding the sentence. If you want a slow pace (and occasionally that is the case for something academic or intellectual) then you will be all right with the passive voice. If, however, you want your story to move along more quickly, stick with the active voice.

(Note that the terms *active voice* and *passive voice* are not related to the term *voice* as used to define how your story sounds to the reader.)

Theme

The theme of your story is its underlying message. In longer stories, especially, theme becomes an important factor in what the story communicates to the reader.

To better understand theme, when you finish a first draft of a story, ask yourself, "What is this story really about?"

Is it about redemption, or forgiveness, or true love, or hate? There are many possible themes, but a good story usually has just one, though occasionally some minor themes play successfully off the story's main theme.

Theme usually emerges from your story as you write. In many cases, you won't know what the real theme is until you have finished the first draft. Then, as you revise, you become aware of your theme. Once you work out what the theme is, make sure in the revision process that the various elements of the story all contribute to that theme, and don't work against it.

For instance, the theme of Greg Couch's story about boxer Steve Langley (see Appendix A) might be described as perseverance despite a lack of respect. How does Couch's choice of anecdotes work to support that theme?

Take a look at the anecdote about Langley's efforts to lose weight before the fight. What does that anecdote say about his perseverance?

If Couch had chosen another anecdote, perhaps one about the boxer's successes in the past, it might not have worked as well to support the theme and the story might have started to wander. In his revision process, Couch had twice as much story as there was space available. To make the story fit, he carefully chose those exact anecdotes, those exact metaphors and similes, those exact pieces of description that worked best for a tightly written, effective story. Note also that an additional benefit of increased precision was a heightened sensitivity to the subject, which inevitably increases the appeal of the article to its readers. (See Chapter 11.)

You will want to do the same.

Exercises

1. How would you describe the voice and tone of Sherry Long's travel story on Edinburgh, Scotland (reprinted in Appendixes B and C)? If an editor asked Long to

make the story even more personal, describe in a few para-graphs what kind of changes she could make that would change the story's voice?

2. Try rewriting the opening page of Sherry Long's story in an institutional voice and then compare it with the final draft as reprinted. Discuss in a few paragraphs why travel stories are often written in a more personal voice.

3. What is the theme of Long's story? Can you identify it in a few words? How about Batz's ADD story? Wilber's "Scene on Bayshore" story? Wittwer's story on water-skier Corey Cook?

4. Pair off with another writer. Each of you read the other's story and write down the theme of the piece in one short phrase like "Love conquers all," or "Hard work brings rewards," or "Flirting is fun." Hand the stories back and see if the theme is what you thought it was as you wrote the piece. If it isn't, what parts confused your reader? Talk it over. If it *is* what you meant it to be, ask your reader what parts made that clear.

CHAPTER

6

Your Final Draft

When you are ready to turn in the final, revised draft of your story, appearances start to matter. Especially if you are freelancing, your writing must look professional and polished as it competes with dozens or hundreds of other stories for the editor's attention. A manuscript that doesn't conform to the accepted standards on format and style is not likely to impress a harried editor, especially one with a large stack of other stories to choose from.

Similarly, whether you are a freelancer or a staff writer, a story riddled with errors in spelling, punctuation, capitalization, agreement, or the like is unlikely to impress your editor, no matter how brilliant the content. Sloppy writing, in the eyes of the editor, is indicative of sloppy reporting, and casts doubts on the overall merits of your story.

"Spelling and grammar mistakes announce that you're not a professional, that your skills aren't very good," says Sarah Beavers, assistant editor of *Student Leader* magazine, a publication that uses a lot of freelance material from beginning writers.

"The truth of the matter is, if you send us something full of mistakes in typing and spelling, we won't even take a look at it. If it's a query, we'll just reject it, no matter how good the idea is. If it's a cover letter, we won't even take a look at the manuscript. And if it's a manuscript, we won't get past reading the first few paragraphs. We just don't have time for that, when it looks like you're not professional."

In your earlier revisions you probably didn't worry too much about many of these things. A misspelling here and there in the first or second draft of a story is meaningless, because you share that draft only with yourself and a select reader or two.

But when you work on the final draft, the rules change. Now you must find a way to catch these mistakes, fix them, and then produce a final manuscript that is top-notch not only in content, but also in presentation.

How do you go about cleaning up these things in your final draft?

The first step is usually to use the spell-checker on your word processor to help catch spelling problems. It's worth noting, however, that even for problems in spelling your spell-checker can't do a perfect job—the English language is far too tricky for that. The following passage, for instance, would sail right through a typical spell-checker without requiring you to make any corrections:

> Driver John Doe new their were problems on witch car to
> chews for that days race. Won car was faster, but the other
> had butter handling.

As you can see, if a sentence like this is in the opening of your story on the Daytona 500, your software's spell-checker is not likely to save you from almost certain rejection. The spell-checker—and even a grammar-checking software package if you have one—is just the first of several steps you have to take to clean up your manuscript.

The next step is to do a line edit on your story. Look back at Chapter 1 of this book and remind yourself of some of the techniques that will help you do an effective line edit of your own work; then get at it, looking specifically for errors in such things as spelling, capitalization, misplaced modifiers, and agreement. Also keep a sharp eye out for unacceptable shifts in tense or person.

Problem Areas

It is outside the scope of this book to teach you all of the rules of grammar and style that you need to know for effective writing. We can, however, highlight some common trouble spots and give you some advice on sources you can go to for more grammar and style help.

During a line edit, there are several problem areas that you can look for.

Misplaced Modifiers

Among the most common grammatical problems that beginning (and some veteran) writers run into are those that have to do with misplaced modifiers. Dangling participles head this list. A *dangling participle* is a phrase that is placed in front of the wrong word in the sentence. For instance:

> Sprinting for the goal line, the last-minute touchdown was Petersen's fourth on the day.

What that sentence actually means is that the "last-minute touchdown" was doing the sprinting. The writer meant to say Petersen was doing the sprinting, but to do that the writer would have to move the words around so the sentence looks like this:

> Sprinting for the goal, Petersen tried for his fourth touchdown on the day.

These participial phrases can get tricky, giving you shades of meaning that you may not want, so be careful with them. The "ing" words such as gerunds and participles can be tricky to use effectively, so many writers just try to avoid them.

In addition to dangling participles, there are a number of other ways to run into trouble with misplaced modifiers. Many of these wind up being sources of humor, like this one:

> The puppy walked right up to Jane as Greg noticed that she was dirty and her ribs showed through her skin.

Poor Jane.

Spelling and Capitalization

As we noted earlier, spelling is a problem that you can't simply solve with your software's spell-checker. One of the problems that you may face if your spelling is really shaky is that you don't realize the problem, and so you will have a difficult time fixing it. In this case, you will need to find someone with good spelling skills to proofread your story for you.

A good idea is for you to note the mistakes that person finds (and thank him or her profusely) and make a solid effort to learn from them. In many cases, you will soon be able to pinpoint certain words that you consistently misspell. List them (listing both your wrong spelling and the correct one), and then you can do a search in each story for those particular words. Do this often enough and your spelling will improve. Exhibit 6.1 includes a list of 70 commonly misspelled words. You might locate the ones here that are problematic for you, and start your own list today.

Capitalization is much like spelling in that writers who have problems with it are unlikely to fix them until they get help. If that's you, get help. The capitalization issue, however, is made more confusing by the frequency with which it changes according to the particular style of a publication. Some magazines may capitalize job titles when they stand alone (like President or Pope), while others follow the basic Associated Press style and keep those titles lowercase.

The best thing you can do is get to know the particular style decisions of the publication that you want to write for, and meet those expectations.

Generally, there are five main areas of capitalization usage where freelancers and staff writers run into trouble. Here they are, along with a brief explanation of the correct use:

1. A complete sentence inside quote marks begins with a capital letter even though it is in the middle of another sentence.

2. Proper nouns are capitalized and common nouns are not. This can occasionally get tricky, because the accepted style varies, for instance, from *German shepherd* to *french doors.* Your best bet is to look it

E X H I B I T   6 . 1

Commonly Misspelled Words

accommodate	occasion
accumulate	occur/occurred/occurrence
assassinate	omission
beginning	parallel
conceive	pastime
commitment	percent
criticize	persistent
descent	playwright
desirable	possession
doughnut	privilege
embarrass	query
environment	questionnaire
eyeing	readable
fluorescent	receipt
fulfill	receive
genealogy	recommend
grammar	recur/recurrence
height	rhyme
hysterical	rhythm
illegitimate	sacrilegious
inconvenience	seize
independent	separate
judgment	sheriff
knowledgeable	skiing
laboratory	supersede
leisure	teen-age
liaison	tobacco
library	traveler
likelihood	trying
maintenance	usable
manageable	vacuum
maneuver	weird
missile	wield
newsstand	withhold
noticeable	X ray

up, and even then a particular publication may handle it differently. Names, of course, are capitalized, but job titles are usually not unless they directly precede the person's name. So, it is "Professor Jane Jones" when it precedes, but "Jane Jones, a professor," when it follows or stands alone.

Again, this may vary from publication to publication.

3. Trademark names are always capitalized, though their use may have slipped into nearly generic use. Words and phrases such as *Xerox, Kleenex, Scotch tape,* and *Velcro* require the capital letter. If you want to avoid the capital, use a different, completely generic, term such as *cellophane tape,* for instance, in place of *Scotch tape.*

4. Regions of the country are capitalized, but directions are not. So, "We live in the Midwest," and "We go to see a Western movie," but "Head north up I-55," and "Head south to get to Florida."

There are a number of other tricky issues in capitalization, including government bodies (generally capitalized only if they refer to the specific body, like the Senate), academic departments (usually not capitalized unless they are already a proper noun, so write the "Spanish department," and the "history department"), and more.

The rules vary, so if you have any doubts, look it up. Several good sources will help you acquire the basic grammatical and spelling skills that you need. A few of them are:

1. Brian Brooks and James L. Pinson, *Working with Words* (St. Martin's Press, New York).

2. Norm Goldstein, ed., *The Associated Press Stylebook and Libel Manual* (The Associated Press, Reading, Massachusetts).

3. Jay Silverman, Elaine Hughes, and Diana Roberts Wienbroer, *Rules of Thumb: A Guide for Writers* (McGraw-Hill, New York).

4. William Strunk, Jr., and E. B. White, *The Elements of Style* (Macmillan Publishing, New York).

Punctuation

Figuring out where to put the commas and knowing when to use a semicolon or colon are among the most troublesome problems many beginning writers face. Punctuation, after all, is one of the trickiest parts of the language, and one where there are many disagreements in style between the worlds of fiction and nonfiction and the world of academic and popular writing.

Still, editors have every right to expect that you know the basics of punctuation, and by the time you finish revising your manuscript and send it off to your editor, you will need to have your commas, especially, under firm control.

There are many areas of comma usage where both freelancers and staff writers run into trouble. Here are several basic ones, along with a brief explanation of the correct use.

1. Use a comma when you use "said" in front of a direct quote that is a complete sentence on its own. For example: Peter said, "I believe that this letter explains everything."

2. When you list a series of items, use the comma to separate them, up to the last item. If that last item is preceded by a conjunction, don't use the comma. So, write "Samantha received catalogs from Harvard, Yale, Princeton and Brown."

   If, however, the lack of a final comma can make the sentence confusing, then use it. So, write "Samantha received catalogs from Duke, Virginia, and William and Mary." In this case you need the comma to avoid confusion. Note, however, that some publications prefer the final comma regardless. Whenever possible, check the publication's preferences.

3. When you use an introductory word, phrase, or clause, you need the comma after the word, phrase,

or clause. So, write "The student government advisor approved the purchase, and so did the president."

The same holds true for participles, so write "Treading water, John survived for four hours before being rescued."

4. When you use nonrestrictive words, phrases, or clauses, you must use the comma. When you use restrictive words, phrases or clauses, do not use the comma.

This one is not as tricky as it seems. An easy way to see if a word, phrase, or clause is nonrestrictive is to see whether it is essential to the meaning of the sentence by dropping it from the sentence as you read it (or putting it into parentheses). If the sentence still makes sense, then it is nonrestrictive, so use the commas.

For example, "Jamie Douglas, the quarterback, lost the game when he fumbled."

You can see that the phrase "the quarterback" is not essential (and so it is nonrestrictive) and could be dropped, so set it off with commas.

Agreement

Far too many writers have trouble with noun/pronoun and subject/verb agreement, which is puzzling, because this is one area where the rules are fairly straightforward. Simply put, the noun and its pronoun must agree in gender (male or female or neither), number (singular or plural) and person (first, second, or third). Similarly, the subject of a sentence and the verb of the sentence must agree in number. This sometimes gets a bit confusing with collective nouns. Here is a brief discussion of each type of agreement problem.

Noun/Pronoun Problems

In noun/pronoun agreement issues, the important thing is to make clear what is the pronoun's antecedent (the noun to which the pronoun refers is its antecedent). So, in this sentence, "If a student is late for this examination, they will be penalized a full grade point," the "they" is wrong, because the antecedent is "student," which is singular. The pronoun should be "he or she." If that sounds clumsy to you, simply use the antecedent again and say "If a student is late for this examination, the student will be penalized a full grade point."

Hint: It is the use of "they" when the antecedent is singular that seems to crop up the most often in noun/pronoun problems, so be wary. Try looking hard at each use of "they" in your story, and make sure it's a correct usage before you print out your final draft.

Remember, also, that collective nouns most often take the singular pronoun in American-style English (they take the plural in British-style English). So, "The city council voted that it wanted to have more time for discussion." The "it" is correct, and should not be "they."

Similarly, it should be the "The team won its games," not "their" game. Sportswriters often seem to have trouble with this.

The rule on collective nouns is that they always take the singular pronoun unless the use of the collective seems specifically plural in its use. So, "The team pulled on their socks before the game," is correct.

A relatively new trouble spot for sportswriters is the collective nickname, such as the Crimson Tide, the Green Wave, the Lightning, the Storm, the Attack, and the like. Newspaper usage varies on these from paper to paper, so look it up and see what your editor prefers.

Plural sports nicknames are easier, because they always take the plural pronoun. So, "The Bulls won their game" is the correct use of "their."

Subject/Verb Agreement

Basically, the number (singular or plural) of the verb should always agree with the number of the subject, even when there are words or phrases between them. So, "Sunday's game, of the past fifteen games, is the biggest of the season for the Rams." The verb "is" needs to be singular to agree with the subject "game."

One of the trickier phrases that can be inserted and confuse the issue is a prepositional phrase, such as this: "Only one of the quarterbacks has the chance to start the game." The singular "has" is correct, though it follows the plural "quarterbacks," because the actual subject here is "one."

Also, when you connect two or more items in a subject, you make it plural, so "Apples and oranges are on the plate" is correct, because "are" is plural. The exception is when the connected items are thought of as a single thing, like "pork and beans."

Shifts in Person, Tense, or Point of View

Another common trouble spot for beginners and some veteran writers is shifts in person, tense, or point of view. Basically, it is a matter of consistency. For the most part, once you choose first person (I), second person (you) or third person (he, she, or they) for your story, you have to stick with it or you will confuse the reader. Similarly, if you write your story in the present tense, you have to stick with that, too, though you can include flashbacks in past tense. Once you choose a point of view (that is, the person the story follows), you have to stick with it, as well.

You can shift from time to time in each of these things, but the shifts have to be done with a transition that makes it clear to the reader that the shift has occurred. Here are some examples from each of these three problem areas:

Person

Once you have chosen to write in the third person, say, for your story, it is confusing to the reader to shift into first or second person unless there is a transitional break. If your first ten paragraphs have been in third person ("Jane went to the meeting expecting a raise") and then you suddenly shift into second person ("You can imagine how she felt when she was fired"), you confuse the reader, who wasn't being talked to directly ("you" talks directly to the reader) until you suddenly shifted.

The key here, as in so many areas of revision, is consistency. If you establish early on in a story that it is a first-person and second-person blend, you can make that work. The same is true with first and third or second and third person. In each case, though, you need to establish that as your style right off the bat.

Tense

One of the more common areas for beginners to confuse their readers is with tense shifts, and once again this is a matter of consistency. Once you have started your story in the past tense, it is very confusing to suddenly have it jump forward into present tense.

It *is* possible to start in the present tense, as we have said, and go into past-tense flashbacks, but these flashbacks should be used sparingly.

A good technique that allows for a blend of present and past tenses is the block style. See more about that in Chapter 3.

Point of View

Your point of view is the character through which the story is being told—the main character in your story. It confuses the reader to shift from that person's point of view to another unless there is a transition that makes it clear to the reader that a shift has occurred.

Take a look at this passage, for instance.

> Jonathan mowed the grass with the old mower despite his father's warning that the right front wheel seemed loose. It seemed to Jon to be working fine.
>
> The engine was sputtering. Peter cranked it again and again, but the car wouldn't start.

The sudden shift in point of view from Jonathan to Peter confuses the reader, who thinks, at first, that it must be Jonathan's engine that is sputtering.

If you use a transition to begin that second paragraph ("Clear across town, Peter cranked. . .") you can accomplish this point-of-view shift with a great deal less confusion. Your readers, and your editors, will thank you.

Format

Once you have cleared up any stylistic problems (even if just a few per page, they do add up), you can turn your attention to the much simpler task of using an appropriate format for your manuscript. This is something that you don't have to worry about until your final draft, but once you decide that you are ready to show your work to an editor, it needs to meet the editor's expectations for what a manuscript should look like.

The first page of your manuscript should look like the example in Exhibit 6.2.

For freelancers, it is especially important to include your name, address, phone numbers, and Social Security number. The address and phone numbers are so the editor can contact you with the good news that your story has been accepted for publication (or maybe just needs a little revision here and there). The Social Security number is something the editor needs to pay you.

The second page of your manuscript should look something like the page shown in Exhibit 6.3.

Manuscripts that come in single-spaced, or without adequate margins, or, heaven forbid, handwritten, make life difficult for the editor, and that's the last thing any writer wants to do.

Some Final Hints

Here are a few more common problems in addition to those already discussed in this chapter. It is a good idea to make the same sort of list for these problems that you have for your spelling problems, and then check each story for those things you know give you trouble. Don't be surprised if some of the following are on your list:

> 1. **a/an.** It's the sound, not the spelling, of the word following a/an that determines which one you use. So, it's "an" honorable decision, and it's "a" hairy monster. If the sound is a consonant, use "a." If the sound is a vowel, use "an."

E X H I B I T   6 . 2

Sample Manuscript, First Page

```
Rick Wilber
1234 Beach Drive
St. Louis, MO 63122
work: (314) 555-1212
fax: (314) 555-1212
SS#: 000-00-0000


                    SEARCHING FOR TERMS


     Sit down at your computer keyboard, move that
mouse around some on its pad, click on an icon or two
and log onto a good data base. Now, type in a few
search terms that have to do with education and its
use of emerging technologies.
     If that didn't make any sense to you, just ask
your children for some help. They'll know what it
means, and almost certainly be able to help. More
than 97 percent of American elementary schools and
high schools have computers for student use these
days,¹ so you can bet your children are comfortable—
probably a lot more comfortable than you are—with the
digital future. To them, a mouse is a device you use
to move a cursor around on a computer screen, and the
idea of using particular search terms to dive into a
data base seems quite the ordinary way to do a little
research for that high school term paper.

¹ The World Almanac and Book of Facts, 1994
Source: "Searching for Terms," World&I magazine, a
publication of the Washington Times, May 1994.
```

EXHIBIT 6.3

Sample Manuscript, Second Page

Wilber/Search/2

For your search about the new technologies and their impact on our children's education, try terms like "elementary and education and technology," or "elementary or secondary and technology," or, if you want to narrow things down some, add the words "future and quality" or the catch-phrase "multi-media" to the search. Anything similar to those terms should do, anything that will jog the enormous memory of the data base.

Wait a few seconds, and watch what comes up on the screen. When I tried the first few terms recently on NEXIS (a leading data base, one that collects full text from thousands of newspapers, magazines and other sources), I confined the search to recent magazine articles and still had more than 1,000 "hits," or stories where the terms were used. Narrowing the search by adding the terms that talked about quality and the future narrowed things down some, but there were still hundreds of hits.

Not only does my little exercise in modern research show how quick and effective a data base search can be these days, it also shows how hot this topic is. Educators nationwide are working hard to find the best ways to make use of the new technologies to improve the way we teach our children.

We all know the bad news—the horrific anecdotes and statistics of violence and fear in some schools,

Source: "Searching for Terms," *World&I* magazine, a publication of the *Washington Times*, May 1994.

---

2. **affect/effect.** *Affect* is the verb, *effect* is the noun, unless the verb means "to bring about," in which case use *effect* as the verb. So, write "Roberta can effect change" and "Roberta has a strong effect on the program," but write "She really has affected us."

3. **among/between.** *Among* means you are in the middle of three or more things ("among the crowd in section A"). *Between* means between two at a time ("Odysseus was between a rock and a hard place.")

4. **compose/comprise.** When you create, you "compose." It also means "to put together," and can be used passively, as in "The university is composed of five colleges." When you contain, you "comprise," as in "The university comprises five colleges."

5. **different than.** Avoid this, and use "different from" instead, so "Jane is different from her twin in many ways."

6. **farther/further.** Physical distance is "farther," as in "The castle is farther down the road." More time or degree is "further," as in "I will study the issue further."

7. **fewer/less.** Use "fewer" when the items can be thought of as individuals, use "less" when there are no separate items. So, write "This radio station plays fewer commercials" (you can think of individual commercials) and "This pool has less water," (you can't picture individual water).

8. **hanged/hung.** The past tense of a hanging as an execution is "hanged," so write "He was hanged for the crime." Otherwise, use "hung" for the past tense of "hang."

9. **hopefully.** Your best bet is to avoid this word, because it is so commonly misused. "Hopefully, we will win the game," actually means that we will win the game with hope. What the writer meant to say was "We hope we will win the game."

10. **imply/infer.** Writers "imply" something in the words they use. Readers "infer" something from those words.

11. **its/it's.** The contraction *it's* only means "it is." The possessive form is *its*. If you never use the contraction (using "it is" instead), you will never make this mistake.

12. **lay/lie.** This pair is a toughie, so look it up if you are unsure. Basically, *lay* is the action word, and *lie* is the state of reclining or the telling of something untrue.

13. **like/as.** *Like* is a preposition, as in "Jane swims like a fish." *As* is a conjunction, as in, "Jane swims as well as she should for her level."

14. **raise/rise.** You "raise" animals or things, and "rear" people. You "rise" in the morning from your bed.

15. **split infinitives.** Many editors don't want any words coming between *to* and its verb in an infinitive phrase, so you should say "I love to eat fish," and not throw in a modifier, as in "I love to quickly eat fish." Split infinitives seem to be increasingly acceptable, though.

16. **that/which.** *That* introduces an essential clause, and *which* introduces a nonessential clause. So, write "The caboose is the car that ends the train," or "The caboose, which ends the train, came last."

17. **unique.** This means "the only one of its kind," and is so commonly misused that you are best to avoid it. Usually the writer meant "unusual" when he or she wrote "unique." You cannot be "pretty unique" or "nearly unique," or "really unique."

18. **who/whom.** *Who* is the subject of the action, *whom* is the object, so write "Who won the game?" or "The game was won by whom?"

19. **who's/whose.** Like the it/it's problem, you can avoid this one entirely if you never use the contraction for "who is." *Whose* is the possessive, *who's* is only the contraction for "who is."

20. **you're/your.** *You're* is the contraction for "you are," and *your* is the pronoun. Again, if you avoid the contraction, you can avoid this problem.

Exercises

1. Which of the following words is/are spelled incorrectly? Find the incorrect spellings and correct the mistake.

accomodate	independant
assasinate	newstand
committment	pasttime
desireable	playwrite
embarass	priviledge
enviroment	reciept
occured	seperate
grammer	useable

2. Use as many of the words from the above list as you can—and spell them incorrectly—in a few paragraphs of copy describing the assassination of a world leader. Trade that list with a colleague and see how well that writer does in identifying the errors. How well did you do with his or her similar passage?

3. Do a similar exercise with common errors in capitalization and agreement. Create a mistake-filled two-paragraph passage, and then trade with another writer to correct each other's mistakes.

7

Tightening and Lengthening

In several places in this book, we talk about tight writing. Veteran writers and editors know that the revision process often involves finding ways to get rid of unnecessary words, sentences, paragraphs, blocks, or even sections, because tightly written stories are more likely to hold the reader's interest by presenting a steady stream of entertaining and informative material. Stories that are loosely constructed, on the other hand, slow the reader down with material that doesn't directly serve the purpose of the story. Loosely constructed stories are, in fact, unlikely to see print, because the great majority of editors want clean, tight copy from their writers.

What you will want to do, then, is make sure that your final draft is as tight as it can be, with every word contributing to the story's appeal for the reader.

Tightening Your Writing

Several techniques will help you tighten your copy.

Get Rid of Redundancies

Some redundancies are obvious, some not quite so obvious. Here is an obvious one: "John sauntered slowly down the lane." The word "sauntered" means to walk slowly, so, unless the writer actually means to walk *very* slowly (a slow saunter), the adverb "slowly" is redundant.

Here is another obvious one: "At last, the Reno police finally caught up with the fugitive."

"At last" and "finally" say the same thing in this sentence, so one of them needs to go. A better sentence would be, "The Reno police finally caught up with the fugitive."

You can see that it is often adverbs that are unnecessary in a sentence. Keep an eye on your adverbs and make sure they are really needed every time you use one.

Here is a redundancy that is a bit trickier: "The music rose and the skaters came back on the ice as the intermission ended."

This story had previously made it clear that intermission was taking place, so the phrase "as the intermission ended," is redundant. Clearly, if the skaters are back, the intermission is over.

Here are two more that sound all right at first, but can be tightened: "John Jones was named starting quarterback of the football team."

And, "John Jones married his wife 20 years ago."

In the first case, the sentence can end after "quarterback," because "of the football team" is unnecessary to the sentence's meaning. Similarly, in the second case "his wife" is unnecessary. Who else would John Jones marry, if not his wife?

Say It Simply

Beginning writers often use words that are not necessary to a sentence's meaning. Writers who try to cram too much into each sentence inevitably wind up with murky, long-winded sentences that find very little appeal with editors. What you want to strive for, instead, is to say things simply and directly.

Take a look at this sentence:

> The reason John Jones gave for quitting his job was that he was feeling sick.

Now look at that same thought expressed this way:

> John Jones quit because of illness.

You can see the second version expresses the same idea, but does it in six words instead of fifteen. That kind of simple, straightforward language is easier for the reader to follow, and economy of writing also allows you to get more said in each story, despite the length limitations an editor may place on the story.

Along these same lines, writing in the passive voice adds unnecessary words to the sentence, and also forces the reader to reconstruct the sentence into active voice to figure out its meaning.

For example:

At 4 P.M., the burning house was reached by the firefighters.

This passive voice sentence not only uses more words to express the idea, it forces the reader to reconstruct it into this sentence:

The firefighters reached the burning house at 4 P.M.

You are almost always better off with a straightforward active voice construction that follows a subject, verb, object pattern.

Avoid Unnecessary Gerunds and Participles and Forms of the Verb "to Be"

Two of the most common ways that beginning writers add unnecessary words to sentences, and so slow down the reader, is through the use of gerunds and participles and forms of the verb "to be."

Look at this sentence:

Michael Jordan was playing defense well and also scored 29 points.

If you get rid of the gerund phrase ("playing defense") and let the verb form stand on its own, the sentence reads as follows:

Michael Jordan played defense well and also scored 29 points.

Forms of the verb "to be," often in tandem with gerunds, generally make for weak verb construction in a sentence. Use a strong verb, instead of a weak half-noun, half-verb (which is what a gerund is).

Here are a few more examples:

> There are 15 books that discuss that topic.

> O'Neil's criticism of the movie was unusually harsh.

> The reason for this memorandum is to offer several suggestions to management.

By getting rid of the "is/was" verbs, those sentences become:

> Fifteen books discuss that topic.

> O'Neil harshly criticized the movie.

> This memorandum offers management several suggestions.

In each case, the revised version uses fewer words and yet more directly expresses the idea.

Avoid Unnecessary Modifiers

Closely tied to any discussion of nouns and verbs is the use of unnecessary modifiers. Find strong nouns and verbs, rather than using many adjectives and adverbs to make weak nouns and verbs more specific or descriptive. Words such as *very* and *pretty* are fuzzy in their meaning and annoying to the reader.

Take a look at these sentences:

> John Jones was very upset when he found out.

> John Jones was pretty upset when he found out.

In each of these sentences, the reader struggles to understand exactly what is meant. How upset is "very" upset? How upset is "pretty" upset? The reader can't know for sure. A better way to write that sentence is:

> John Jones was furious when he found out.

Adjectives modify nouns, and so have their uses. But many beginning writers rely too much on the modifiers and not enough on finding exactly the right noun. If you can find the right noun and cut back on the number of adjectives you use, you will produce tighter, better stories.

This version of a sentence from Jeannette Batz's story on attention deficit disorder shows what can happen when you let your adjectives take over:

> Getting your close, personal friends to really get a good understanding of it is pretty easy, but high-school or middle-school teachers can be a little more difficult to educate.

Here is Batz's final version of that sentence. This version cuts out a number of the modifiers, yet still maintains the right voice for a *Seventeen* article:

> Getting your friends to understand is fairly easy, but teachers can be a little harder to educate.

You can see that "close," "personal," "really," "get a good," "pretty," "high-school or middle-school" and "more difficult" can all be eliminated or replaced with a single, better word.

That is the kind of writing you want to work toward, where the single best word replaces the not-quite-right phrase.

Avoid Cliches

Cliches, those overworked expressions that readers see all too often, lose their impact through overuse. The phrase "bitter end," for example, should carry with it a real sense of bitterness, but it no longer does because it has become a cliche.

Some cliches are comparisons that have been overused, others are images or just old sayings. Your writing will improve when you go through your story and delete the cliches or change them to something more original. Here is a short list of common cliches:

all things considered	drastic action
ample opportunity	drunk as a skunk
apples and oranges	easier said than done
awesome	exception proves the rule
better late than never	food for thought
bitter end	fought like a tiger
bolt from the blue	generation gap
by leaps and bounds	grave concern
cold as ice	heated argument
cool network	hot and heavy
crying need	join the club
dire need	leaves much to be desired

madly in love   ripe old age
marked contrast   raining cats and dogs
moment of truth   sweeping changes
narrow escape   slept like a log
old hat   smooth as silk
one and the same   wined and dined

Just Say "Said"

Beginning writers sometimes feel the need to use descriptive words or phrases to connect a quote with its source, as in: "I'm so sorry it happened that way," Elizabeth moaned.

"Moaned" seemed a good idea to this student writer because it conveyed a particular kind of statement. The problem comes from attaching a word like "moaned" to every quote in a story. The emotions quickly run wild and the reader is just as quickly annoyed. Take a look at the following passage:

> "I really wanted to come along," Joan cried, "but John made it clear I wasn't allowed."
> "Oh, it's all right," Joe muttered.
> "But what will John do? He'll be upset, I'm sure," Joan moaned.
> "We'll deal with that when we get there," whispered Joe.

You can see that the scene becomes filled with overwrought characters crying, muttering, moaning, and whispering. Imagine page after page with this sort of dialogue. To avoid this problem, use "said," in almost all cases. "Said" is invisible to readers, and simply serves as a visual cue to establish the source of a quote. As a result, "said" is a word that is difficult to overuse, unlike virtually all of its replacements.

You may, on occasion, want to use an alternate word ("says," in the present tense, is more commonly used these days), but be sparing in that use. See how the previous passage reads with "said" in place of all the moaning and crying.

> "I really wanted to come along," Joan said, "but John made it clear I wasn't allowed."

"Oh, it's all right," Joe said.

"But what will John do? He'll be upset, I'm sure."

"We'll deal with that when we get there," said Joe.

You can see the characters seem less overexcited, and what they say comes through to the reader more clearly without the long list of emotionally loaded words.

In general, in tightening your story make sure that every word, every block, and every section is doing its job.

Lengthening a Story

Remember, though, that tight writing doesn't necessarily mean short writing. It is likely that in the revision process you will tighten up the piece throughout, but also add new material that actually lengthens the story.

That is not as odd as it sounds at first. Tight writing means that every word counts in each sentence and paragraph you write. Any words that don't contribute to the story's success are edited out.

Even a very long story, however, can be built from a series of tightly written sentences, paragraphs, blocks, and sections. If each element is tightly constructed and the transitions connecting them are subtle and effective, the story moves along nicely no matter its length.

There are times, in fact, that you will have to write longer than you would like on a particular story. In newspaper and magazine writing, and often in public relations writing, as well, the editor sometimes needs a story of a given length to fit into a page design that is ready for it.

If the editor wants a story from you that is 2,500 words long, and yours has only 2,000, you can expect to have the editor ask for a revision that comes in at the required 2,500-word mark. The trick is to lengthen the piece without weakening it.

Some hints on how to write tightly, but still lengthen a story when the need arises, follow.

Use More Quotes

This technique works well, but only when you use it without cluttering the story up with repetition. It is important to remember that the quotes you add must provide new information or expand usefully on previously supplied information. If you just repeat what is found in other quotes or information blocks, the story bogs down for the reader.

For example, if this is the original quote:

> "Well, it seems like the metro area receives enough rainfall to meet our need. But, many of those 50 inches of annual rain come in summer thunderstorms, and much of that water drains away before it has a chance to percolate into the aquifer," said Miller.

Then this expansion will just slow the reader down:

> "Well, it seems like the metro area receives enough rainfall to meet our need. But, many of those 50 inches of annual rain come in summer thunderstorms, and much of that water drains away before it has a chance to percolate into the aquifer," said Miller.
>
> Leslie agreed. "Sure, that's our primary problem. Most of those summer rains never make it into the aquifer to replenish it," he said.

You can see that the second quote repeats the information in the first quote, providing nothing for the reader. You might get away with this sort of lengthening once or twice, but if you try it very often, readers will soon catch on to the repetition and will find the story slow going.

On the other hand, if you follow the first quote with another one that provides new, useful information, the lengthening works better for the reader.

> "Well, it seems like the metro area receives enough rainfall to meet our need. But, many of those 50 inches of annual rain come in summer thunderstorms, and much of that water drains away before it has a chance to percolate into the aquifer," said Miller.
>
> "And it's not just the summer rains draining away uselessly that's the problem," said Leslie. "There's too much pavement and not enough soil in the metro area, so even the gentle, steady rains can't percolate down into the aquifer."

You can see how the second quote doubles the length of the information presented, and does it with new facts ("too much pavement") that expand on the previous quote's usefulness.

Give Additional Factual Support

Additional information blocks can lengthen a story in much the same way that an additional quote does, but the same warnings apply. It is important that the new information blocks not simply repeat previously presented information. A good way to handle this sort of expansion is to cite a general fact, and then expand usefully on that fact with a good example. For example:

> Parents matter most—their attitude can make or break a daughter's struggle with ADD. "Try harder," is the worst thing you can say to a child with ADD," says Corinne's mom, July Olsen. "It just increases the anxiety."
>
> Dr. Dean Rosen, a St. Louis psychologist and ADD specialist, advises parents to focus on developing their daughter's strengths, instead of trying to correct her "flaws" or the "deficit" in her attention. Parents should not take their daughter's angry outbursts personally, or analyze them while they're happening. Above all, parents should give immediate feedback—and remember that praise often falls on deaf ears, so they'll have to repeat it.

You can see that the second paragraph expands on the first. The second paragraph isn't absolutely necessary to the story, which presents a lot of supportive factual material elsewhere, but it *is* useful in backing up the mother's statement. And it adds nine lines to the story. In fact, you can see that this section could easily support a third paragraph that offered even more factual support, as long as the new information brought some new angle into the discussion.

Use Specific Description

One of the weakest areas for many beginning writers is in their ability to describe. As we discuss in Chapter 5, beginners tend to offer too many general descriptions and not enough specific ones. A good way to lengthen a piece is to do what you should be doing anyway—get specific in your descriptive passages.

Take a look at this simple passage:

> Joe and Jane walked along the path through the trees together one more time before she left for her new assignment.

That gets the job done. But compare it with this longer version.

> In the morning, Joe and Jane walked along the footpath one last time. A late spring snow had fallen overnight, just enough to coat the early buds of the oaks and maples that lined the path with a thin band of white. By the stream, the willow sagged in the wet snow, its branches touching the water. Jane's plane left at noon for her new assignment.

This passage evokes a stronger sense of the sadness of the couple's parting, and utilizes foliage, weather, spring, and water to do it. It is four-and-one-half lines longer, as well.

Use More Anecdotes

The use of additional anecdotes to lengthen a story can also work well, if they are relevant and not repetitious.

Anecdotes, as you know from the discussion in Chapter 2, help make the story more effective for the reader by providing a sense of storytelling inside the story, bringing real people into the story and putting them into action.

Anecdotes are easy to overdo, so be cautious when you use them to lengthen a piece. If you use too many anecdotes, the story may start to sound disjointed, more like a connected series of smaller stories than the smooth whole you want it to be.

Still, if you have only used one or two anecdotes in a story, and you need a few more paragraphs of length, an additional anecdote may do the job. Just make sure that the new anecdote contributes something useful to the story, doesn't wander away from your theme, and is not repetitive.

You might try connecting the new anecdote closely to one you have already used, and have it expand on the theme presented in the first anecdote. A simple transitional phrase such as "Another time, Jones . . ." or "Just a month later, Jones had it happen again, when . . ." should allow you to smoothly connect the new addition with the first anecdote.

Exercises

1. See if you can edit this 51-word passage into a passage of 25 words or less that conveys the same information:

> All things considered, I would join the club and say Jamie Clark won his heated debate with Jane Donovan. Smooth as silk, he carefully and cautiously built his facts and figures into a statement that showed the dire need of our school for continued financial support from state tax dollar revenues.

2. D. Quentin Wilber's editor has just asked him to lengthen his "Scene on Bayshore" story by six paragraphs. Help him out and write those new six paragraphs for the story. Assume that you have his notes.

3. D. Quentin Wilber's editor has just asked him to cut his "Scene on Bayshore" story by six paragraphs. Help him out and cut those six paragraphs from the story.

4. When you have finished Exercises 2 and 3, trade them with another writer and compare what the two of you have done with the story. Who did the better job? How did he or she accomplish it?

8

Editor
Relationships

Once you have finished the final draft of your story and are
ready to give it to your editor, you may think you are through
with the hard work of revision and are approaching the writer's
payoff, publication.

Well, not so fast. Whether you submitted the story on
speculation, you are a staff writer, or you sent the piece in to
meet a contractual deadline, you are still likely to do significant revising on a story *after* it gets to the editor.

If you have submitted it on speculation, you may find from
time to time that an editor likes the story, but not quite well
enough to buy it as is. In these cases the editor may send you
a note that describes some possibilities for revision. Typically,
the editor will add that he or she would like to see the story
again after you revise it, but will make no firm commitment.
After all, the editor can't be sure that you will be able to revise
suitably.

If you have written the story as work-for-hire (see Chapter
10) for a newspaper or public relations publication, or you
have written it as a freelancer under contract, then the editor
may respond to your final draft with a list of suggested revisions that will, in the editor's eye, help make the story a
success.

Whether you are writing for a newspaper, a magazine, or a public relations outlet, you still have to deal with the editor's needs. From a short newspaper brief or a one-page press release all the way to a lengthy magazine essay (or, for that matter, even a major book), you are likely to be revising one or more times before the story appears in print.

Editors and Editing

From the editor's perspective, revision is just a routine part of the process that takes a story from idea to publication.

Jonathan Cullimore is managing editor of *The Water Skier* magazine, a trade publication published for the American Water Ski Association. Cullimore deals with freelance writers from around the country on a daily basis.

"When we buy a story, we certainly think of that as just the start of the editing process," Cullimore says. "I contact the writer and start to work with that person to formulate the story to our editorial needs. That may take several phone calls and some faxing."

In Cullimore's case, the needs of his magazine are not only those of his readers, as it is for a consumer magazine, but are also the needs of his group's membership, because the magazine is a trade publication of the group. Trade magazines are an aspect of a business's public relations function.

Cullimore says, "We have to satisfy the needs of the American Water Ski Association and our sponsors, too. That's all just part of the job here."

If it is part of Cullimore's job as editor, that makes it part of your job, too, as the writer, so you can expect editing and revisions that will make your story conform to the association's needs.

The Water Skier, like most trade magazines, is an ambitious, slick, high-quality magazine produced by a small staff to serve a large membership. The expectations for accuracy, fairness, design, stylish writing, and entertainment and informational value are at least as critical for trade magazines as they are for national consumer publications such as *Seventeen, Omni,* or others mentioned in this book.

For the story on Corey Cook reprinted in Appendix E, for instance, Cullimore began by receiving a query letter from writer Jennifer Wittwer of Hayward, California. She proposed a story on speed skier Corey Cook.

Cullimore liked the idea, but didn't know anything about Wittwer. So he recalls, "I started by calling her and asking her questions about her connections to waterskiing, just to see if she knew what she was talking about. It turned out she was the girlfriend of the skier she wanted to do that story on. That was fine for us, since that meant she went to all the events and was knowledgeable. That was the key. Did she really keep up with the sport? And, of course, she did."

Because Wittwer was a beginning writer, Cullimore knew he would have a lot of editing work to do when the story reached his desk.

"But she was very easy to work with," Cullimore says, "and that was important. Jennifer was willing to work with me to get the story ready for publication."

As we will discuss later in this chapter, having a writer who is willing to work on revising the story is sometimes very important to an editor. Your attitude matters, whether you are a staffer or a freelancer.

A first draft and a final draft of the story are included in Appendixes D and E. Also included are the additional quotes Cullimore obtained to flesh out Wittwer's story.

For consumer publications, the editor's needs are very similar, in that every magazine has its own narrow focus, and the editor is going to be buying stories that fit that focus.

Put yourself in the place of an editor like Joe Bargmann, senior editor at *Seventeen*. Each workday, Bargmann receives dozens of query letters and manuscripts. There are writers all over the world who want to write for *Seventeen*, so the story proposals and completed manuscripts roll in regularly.

From that stack of query letters and manuscripts, Bargmann finds a few that he thinks will work for *Seventeen*. His response to the successful query letter is usually a note asking the writer to submit the story on speculation, which does not commit him to buying the piece if he doesn't like it. Occasionally, he may ask for a lengthier proposal.

With manuscripts, those rare ones that he buys that just came in over the transom (the usual phrase for unsolicited manuscripts) and, much more frequently, those that he contracted for, there can still be a lot of editing and revision.

"There's always a lot of revising to do," he says. "Writers, especially beginners, have to realize that you just can't get married to your copy. You have to realize that it's malleable. Your story, your words, are your clay, and you've got to form the story out of them, and how you form it at first is not how it's going to end up."

Bargmann's advice for freelancers or staff writers is to remember that you need to hand in the best work you can, but remember, too, that "You have to realize that whatever form you hand it in is not the form it will be published in."

It is worth noting that there are few queries for most trade publications, where the writers most frequently come from within the group, as did the writers of the story on water-skier Corey Cook.

At least three types of editing are undergone by a manuscript *after* it has been accepted for publication by a consumer or a trade magazine.

1. It is edited for grammar and style, including punctuation, capitalization, and the like.
2. It is edited for structure, including the editor's thoughts on how the story flows and how that flow might be improved.
3. It is edited for factual accuracy and legal and ethical concerns.

Editing for Style

When an editor takes your story to edit it for grammar and style, you certainly don't want there to be too many mistakes that he or she can catch.

Each publication, however, has its own particular style when it comes to issues such as capitalization, abbreviations, and even spelling. You are wise to stick with the editor's decisions on those issues, unless it seems to have an impact on the story's content, in which case you need to discuss it with the editor.

For example, "We have quite a few style things that are particular to our magazine," says Kay Quinn King, managing editor of *The Student Leader* magazine. "We capitalize a lot of things that other magazines and newspaper don't, for instance, and we use italics a lot, and some don't do that."

Writers who submit to King's publication "have to meet our style, absolutely," she says. "We'll work with you on it, but it's *our* style, so there's no question about it. And we expect that you'll know these idiosyncracies by the time you write your second piece for us."

In the newspaper business, most papers follow the Associated Press stylebook, but all newspapers have their own variations on that standard AP style, as well. If you are a newspaper staffer or a freelancer, you will be expected to know AP style when you start your job, and to quickly learn your paper's variations including local issues.

The Associated Press stylebook, for instance, says that job titles that stand alone are never capitalized, and that the names of periodicals are not underlined, italicized, or put inside quotation marks, but simply use upper- and lowercase. A sentence combining these two things might look like this:

> The president of the student body insisted that The Daily Collegian was unfair in its coverage of the election.

Note that "president" is lower case, and that the name of the paper is not underlined, italicized, or in quotation marks. Some particular newspapers chose to alter those two style decisions, so it is possible to have the sentence look like this:

> The President of the student body insisted that "The Daily Collegian" was unfair in its coverage of the election.

These changes seem minor, and they are. But they are important to each newspaper, because it is imperative that all reporters and editors for the publication conform to the same rules. Otherwise, the reader would face chaos each day trying to figure out what the paper had in mind.

When you are editing and revising your own story, you will be expected to have these stylistic conventions straight. If you can clean up your own copy before it gets into the hands of your editor, it gives the editor more confidence in you, which is important to you if you are on the staff, and absolutely crucial to you if you are freelancing.

If you can't seem to correct these points of style for yourself as you edit and revise, you can expect to work with your editor to straighten them out. That is a process you don't want to go through too often for this level of editing.

Editing for Structure

When editors look at a story for its structure, they use a variety of techniques to make sure they are comfortable with the way the story flows.

The late Murray Cox, senior editor of *Omni* magazine, was famous for the way he worked with writers on matters of structure.

"When I first look at a feature I'm looking only at the structure," Cox said. "I'm blind to the line work. I want to see where my interest flags, where I get bored, where I start to yawn—so I'm looking for that big stuff at first.

"What I do is outline what a writer gives me, then I begin to see what can be cut, what's superfluous here and there and how the story flows. Sometimes it's very difficult. I worked with one writer whose entire story was driven by just the quotes. The writer didn't see it until I pointed it out, but the article was literally hung together around these characters, and we didn't know anything about the characters because the writer had fallen into the trap where he thought the quotes alone would carry the piece. They didn't."

Cox helped that writer fix the story, bringing in information blocks and narrative. Not all editors are as talented or as helpful as Cox was with writers, but they are all concerned with similar issues. The way a story is built is crucial to the editor's opinion of the piece, and you are likely to find yourself moving blocks and sections around, or writing entirely new ones, to suit the editor's needs.

In Jennifer Wittwer's story on skier Corey Cook, see how a quote block (the third paragraph in the final version) that wasn't in the story at all when editor John Cullimore first saw it, helps validate the writer's statement that Cook is a top competitor.

Fact-Checking

The editing for factual accuracy is usually handled by people called fact-checkers. These are usually entry-level editors and writers at the magazine whose job it is to research every fact, every quote, every spelling of every name in your story. The fact-checker (sometimes grandly called an "editorial assistant") then sends the writer a list of all the changes and corrections, which you can react to by accepting or revising.

It should be a fairly straightforward process, and often there are several of these changes or corrections per page, so don't panic when you see them. Remember that in all cases the fact-checker has called to verify the information you presented, so the questions raised are most likely valid ones.

Every now and then you may find that a source can cause you problems during the revision process by denying a quote when the fact-checker calls. In those rare circumstances, you may find yourself in a touchy discussion with your editor, a discussion that will go best for you if you have a tape recording of the interview, or at least can back up the quotes with your notes from the interview.

Building Trust

One of the most important things you can do as a writer is to build a mutually respectful relationship with editors who will work with you to maximize your story. If you are too sensitive about editing, or if you get a reputation for always needing a lot of editing, you will find the revision process an unnecessarily difficult one.

On the other hand, you need to know when to stand up for a particular passage that you think belongs in the story or needs to be expressed exactly the way you expressed it.

A good piece of general advice is that you should be ready to negotiate from time to time with the editor. Don't fight every small change the editor wants to make, be appreciative of the improvements the editor offers, and you will have some leverage when you want to keep a particular passage exactly the way it is.

What you want to wind up with is a steady relationship with several editors. They need to know they can count on you for clean copy that is accurate, fair, entertaining, and informative.

Mary Batten, editor of the Cousteau Society's magazine *Calypso Log,* says "What I try to do as an editor is build up a stable of writers whom I can count on, whose work I know, whose research I can trust, and who like to work for us. That's the ideal for any editor, to have a group of writers whom you've worked with before, who are thoroughly professional, who meet their deadlines, and do their research well, and whom you can count on."

That is important for any editor, of course, and helps explain why it can be tough for a new writer to break into the market. Editors trust the writers they know.

Jonathan Cullimore, at *The Water Skier,* says much the same thing. "We get regular writers and we like to stick with them. A lot of our training articles are from skiers who train or run ski schools, and they write regularly for us. We learn to depend on them, and they learn just what sort of story we need."

In terms of revision, this means that if you want to break into the group of writers an editor knows and trusts, the first thing you have to do is submit polished, professional stories with the right focus for the magazine. Then, if the editor likes the story but wants revision, happily go about revising and meeting the editor's needs.

Remember that you may not get too many chances with any one editor. Murray Cox said, for example, that "For the most part, I hold to one rewrite. If it doesn't work on the first rewrite—and not all of them do, of course—then it might not work at all."

This same sense of trust, of building a long-term relationship, holds true when you are on a newspaper or magazine staff.

Wichita Eagle assistant sports editor Tom Seals doesn't have to worry about freelancers, but he does have to worry about the pressure of daily deadlines on a number of different writers. If you are interested in newspaper work, you will find that working with editors like Seals is part of the job, and it is a part where you don't have the leisure of taking your time to get the job done, as you sometimes do in magazine or public relations work.

Seals says, "There almost never is enough time to edit daily newspaper copy the way you'd like. In the sports department, where I am, the majority of the stories are written on deadline. What that means, generally, is that when I get my hands on a story, I try to do all the editing at once. I start at the top and head straight down the screen, correcting grammar, style, and spelling (never trust computer spell-checkers), but also slashing lame quotes and, if necessary, rearranging paragraphs as I go."

For Seals, there often is not time to work with a writer when the reporting isn't up to par, so "sloppy reporting usually is corrected simply by chopping out the sloppiness," he says, adding that "It's certainly not the ideal way to go, but it's a fact of life. When the press starts in 45 minutes, you simply have to move fast."

The single major difference between Seals's work and the work of the magazine editors we have talked to is that when an editor works on a newspaper, he or she knows that "Most newspaper reporters are fairly competent," Seals says. "They generally don't need hours of rewriting. They take pride in their stories."

Still, if you want the editor's revisions to be minimal when you are on the staff of a newspaper or a magazine, acquire a reputation as one of the writers who can be trusted.

After all, Seals says, "Naturally, some [of our writers] are more talented than others. We have a couple people on our staff whose copy is pristine, whose story structure is nearly always perfect, and whose stuff should generally be left alone. In fact, there have been a few times when I have gone in and undone the editing of my copy editors."

Doesn't that sound like the way you would like your work to be treated?

Remember that no matter how good you are, or how good you think you are, "No writer is perfect," Seals says. "They all have typos. They all make simple mistakes (your/you're, to/ too, under/less than, like/as if). Each of our writers has personal habits I can't break. One guy uses "of course" at least once in each story. Some do require more work more consistently than others. I've never considered that a problem, though. I like to edit. Those perfect people bore me."

Seals deals primarily with staff sportswriters, but other newspaper editors echo his thoughts.

Janice Hall, for instance, is editor of the "Baylife" feature section of the *Tampa Tribune*. She deals not only with staff writers, but also with a growing list of freelancers. The *Tribune*, like many newspapers, has found that one answer to ever-tightening staff budgets is to buy more freelance material, especially for feature sections, travel sections, and other non-hard-news areas of the newspaper.

"As our salary budget has gotten tighter and our staff has shrunk, we've started using freelancers more and more. I think the trend will continue, too, as newspapers face our uncertain future. It's a good way to keep the costs down and still run quality feature stories."

Newspaper feature writers, whether staff or freelance, quickly learn that writing features is very different, indeed, from writing news.

"The thing with daily newswriting," says Hall, "is that generally your stories are much shorter, and usually they're much more focused: Someone's been killed or a bank has been robbed. The story is really kind of mapped out for you. You can go get the details of what happened, talk to a few people involved, talk to the police, come back and write your eight- to ten-inch story. It's all pretty much formula writing."

With features, on the other hand, Hall says, "You often have to start from scratch. You have to do all the background work, find the sources, check databases and things like that, and only then can you even decide what kind of focus you're going to take."

This means that a real problem area for feature writers, staff or freelance, is focus. As we discussed earlier, sometimes it is only in the writing of the first draft that you realize the focus of the piece, and you then have to stay aimed at that focus when you work on the second and third drafts.

Hall sees a number of other problems that lead to revisions.

"Single-source stories are a real trouble spot," she says. "In the old days, a feature writer could do that. You could see a trend and call one expert and then write the story. Now we want more credibility, so we ask that you call several people for source information.

"Some reporters revert to old habits, I guess, and still turn in single-source stories, so we have to ask for revisions on them."

By the way, if you have trouble with commas or with your spelling, you might like to know that even at a large metro daily newspaper such as the *Tampa Tribune*, "There are reporters who are very prolific, and they're wonderful reporters, but their spelling is atrocious," says Hall.

Those writers get a reputation for spelling problems, Hall points out, which means their copy is scrutinized more closely. That kind of scrutiny means the stories are more likely to be heavily edited, and that the editors have learned not to trust the writer.

In another important point about newspaper editors' revisions, Hall emphasizes that some writers mistakenly equate length with quality.

"Some writers do tend to overwrite," she says. "They mistake quantity for quality, believing that a story can look important if it's long, when in fact it might be dull and boring and the reader is plodding through it."

The truth of the matter is, says Hall, that "Nowadays, people seem to have limited time to sit down and read a newspaper, and the cost of newsprint is high and not going to get any better. We have less of a newshole and therefore we have to write tight. What used to be a 40-inch story now has to be 20 or 25 inches—or even less."

One of Hall's writers has a goal that every good writer should have. "His goal is to have people read to the end of his story," she says, "and that's a great goal."

As discussed earlier, that doesn't mean that every story is a short one—sometimes the subject matter and your writing skill can take a story to great length and still be successful for the reader (and the editor).

"I have one writer here whose copy is wonderful. She's really skilled, each paragraph hooks you into the next one, so when she writes long it's hard to whack."

But that kind of writing takes a lot of skill, and includes a lot of revising to make sure that the flow is constant and smooth, and the material is always engaging, avoiding those valleys that Murray Cox talks about earlier in this chapter.

Don't think that public relations writers don't face these same problems, by the way. Not only are there sometimes extra layers of corporate bureaucracy that need to see and approve the story, the deadline pressures are frequently just as bad as those at a daily newspaper. You need to be able to work quickly and well with an editor in public relations, too.

Lisa Couch, who works for a not-for-profit agency in Wichita, Kansas, says, "Despite the fact that it's public relations, we don't have the luxury of time you might expect. In the non-profit world we do a lot of stuff in a short amount of time, and we do it with a bare-bones staff."

Couch says she wants to keep the revisions to a minimum, but has to balance that against making sure the copy is exactly what she needs.

Most of the writers these editors are talking about in this chapter are writers who have earned the editor's respect. If you are talented and lucky, you will do the same. But that respect is something you have to earn.

As Janice Hall from the *Tampa Tribune* says, "The best advice I can give any beginning writer is to never turn in a story that if someone put it into the paper without being edited you would be embarrassed."

In other words, turn in copy that you are convinced is ready to print, but then don't be surprised when the editor still manages to find things worth revising. Always remember that revision is just part of the process of writing, and try to learn from every story that you publish.

"I think every writer should always read back over the story when it's in print," says Hall. "Many times writers don't do that, I think, and that means they're missing what the editors have done to help the story, and so they aren't learning and aren't getting better." That, Hall knows, is frustrating for an editor, who wants to see the writer improve.

The point is, she says, "Seeing what the editors have done with your story is like getting a test paper back in school. You learn as much from your mistakes as from what you did correctly."

That's a good point.

Once you have established the kind of relationship with an editor that allows for it, one thing you might want to do is have some conversations about the story and its focus before ever handing in your final draft.

This is very common in the magazine business, where those kinds of conversations can save a lot of revising, and they occur daily in newspaper and public relations work, as well.

"I used to be annoyed by reporters who wanted to talk about their stories before they wrote," admits Tom Seals. "I routinely told them to stop telling me about it and just write it. But I've come to realize that when there's time, talking really seems to help. If we spend a few minutes talking about what the story is going to say, what the best quotes are, discussing which direction to go, who else needs to be called—all that talking seems to help the story come together better for the writer."

Seals thinks of himself as a sounding board for his writers in these circumstances. "Sometimes I don't even offer a suggestion," he says, "but, while telling me about his story a reporter will come up with his own new ideas. Since I work evenings, often a reporter will have been working on a story for several hours when I get there, and I can give him a fresh perspective."

These conversations don't always take the formal editor-reporter form. They often work best if it is a friendly chat. The idea is to get you, the writer, to think about what you are writing before you put it down on paper or the computer screen.

Exercises

1. Act like the fact-checker for Jeannette Batz's story on ADD. Make a list of all the quotes, names and facts that you would have to check for the story before it gets into print.

2. Now take a first or second draft of one of your own recent stories and go through the same process, listing all the quotes, names and facts that a fact-checker would verify before the story got into print. As the writer of this piece, are you concerned about the accuracy or fairness of any of these items? Describe how you can address those concerns in the next draft of the story.

3. Using your classmates or your writers' group, have all the writers in the group give their stories to you at once. Assuming there are about a dozen stories, give yourself 30 minutes to rank them from best to worst, using any criteria you like. Describe how much attention you paid to each story. Describe closely what appealed to you about the best stories, and what you didn't like about the worst.

9

Your Writing and the Internet

Been surfing on the Net lately? Find any interesting URLs? If you are in public relations, does your company have a home page, and do you log on daily to check your e-mail? If you are a magazine or newspaper staffer or you are freelancing a story, did your most recent database search get you the information you needed, or did Nexis let you down?

If that first paragraph sounded like technobabble to you, you are not alone. The new technologies that surround us have a lot of writers and editors learning what seems like a whole new language to use and a new set of research, writing, and editing skills.

There is no question that you need these computer-based skills to compete as a writer, and they are just as important to the editing and revision process—in several significant ways—as they are to any other aspect of writing.

For one thing, a growing number of editors and writers converse and otherwise do business through electronic mail (e-mail), handling everything from query letters to actual story submissions and then story revisions. These editors and writers find that e-mail is much cheaper, quicker, and in some key respects more reliable, than the usual postal channels. So, if you want to keep up with the editors' needs, you need to be comfortable with computers and various word processing software packages. You also need to be able to send and receive e-mail and story files through your computer.

As a regular freelancer of fiction and nonfiction for a wide variety of publications, I frequently write stories, revise them, and then send them to the editor, all through a home computer.

More and more frequently, the only time many of these stories see hard copy is when they are in print in the publication or when a hard copy is printed out for use in the revision process. (Why print out a draft? Go back and take another look at Chapter 1).

As the editor of *Fiction Quarterly*, a short-story supplement for a large metro daily newspaper, I sometimes receive stories the same way. Like most editors, I find that for a variety of reasons it still doesn't make sense to receive too many queries or submissions by e-mail, but you will probably find that changing over the next few years as technologies improve.

Even in the case of hard copy submissions, it is common these days for the editor who has bought one of your stories to ask you to send along a copy of that story on disk, so the magazine or newspaper can simply download the story from the disk into the publication's computer and save the time and expense of typing the story in by hand.

At the very least, then, even if you are not able to send and receive material through a modem, you should be able to put your final version of a story onto a disk to send to your editor.

On-line Publications

Freelancers and staff writers for newspapers and magazines have been among the first writers to recognize the importance of the computerized future, not only for publications as they currently exist, but also for the growing number of publications that either have special on-line editions or only exist in an on-line version.

Many publications are already on-line. Some of these magazines and newspapers are available on one of the commercial on-line services such as Prodigy, CompuServe, or America Online. A much larger and rapidly growing number are on the Internet, that loose gathering of computer networks from all over the world.

Once you learn how to access the Internet (and it is quite simple, really, if you have the right hardware and software), you will see how this new method of delivery for magazines gives the publications the ability to cheaply and quickly reach millions of potential readers all over the world.

The business community, too, has been increasingly active on-line, offering corporate home pages (more about home pages later) that include everything from electronic versions of corporate brochures and magazines, to interactive examples of corporate products.

The wise public relations professional understands not only the current needs of this growing market, but also the myriad possibilities for the future.

Many professionals in the field routinely attend conferences where they learn about corporate communications in the information age, focusing on things such as internal and external home pages, electronic newsletters for employees and the public, using computers for on-line research, using computers to communicate through the media, and much more.

It is an exciting future for corporate communicators, and for consumer magazine and newspaper writers, too. Timeliness, for instance, is a major factor in the newspaper business, and an on-line newspaper suddenly has the ability to be as timely as radio and television, with the capability of getting a story into the public's hands (or on the public's computer screens) just as quickly as the writer can write the story, work with an editor to polish it quickly, and then send it out into cyberspace.

However, be warned, Rick Schuerman, editor of *Tampa Bay Online*, the digital edition of the *Tampa Tribune*, points out that the on-line versions of newspapers and magazines bring new demands for writers.

"First," Schuerman says, "the deadline is always 'Now' for an on-line publication. Just as quickly as you can write it, we can get the story out.

"Second, the newshole is infinite. Having enough room to fit a story in is no longer an issue. We can use a story no matter how long it is."

These are two huge shifts in thinking for most newspaper writers. For more than 150 years, newspaper reporters have learned to meet a daily deadline, focusing their workday toward that deadline, knowing that as the deadline approached they would have to stop doing their reporting (even if it was not as complete as they would like) and get started doing their writing.

Also, the wise reporter knew how much space was available that day for his or her story and wrote the story to fit that space. If the story came in too long, it would be cut, and perhaps that close to deadline the cuts wouldn't be those the reporter would have liked. So, it was better to write to fit.

The combination of these two pressures, time and space, has been the single most important factor affecting how newspaper writers have edited and revised their stories for the past century and a half. When you are revising and the deadline hits, you simply have to stop the revision work and send the story in. When you have written a 36-inch story (about six typewritten pages worth) and you are told that only 20 inches are available in that day's paper, your revising becomes focused, of necessity, on cutting the story down to fit rather than revising to improve the piece.

At first glance the limitations of time and space, then, seemed to make life more difficult for the newspaper writer. But, in reality, in many cases these limitations made life easier, allowing the reporter to turn in a story that wasn't everything it could have been but would have to do, under the circumstances.

Now, the circumstances have changed. With on-line newspapers being 24-hour operations (that is, stories can be added, deleted, or changed at any time), the limitations of time and space are gone, and that throws a whole new set of demands at the newspaper writer.

In terms of timeliness, it is increasingly likely that all newspaper (and some magazine) writers may begin to have to learn the revision techniques long practiced by wire service writers, focusing on getting an immediate version of the story into the on-line publication, and then following that with revisions (sometimes called "write-thrus") that expand and clarify the story as more information becomes available.

In terms of length, because there are no space limitations with an on-line publication, you may well find yourself with a story that gets longer and longer as each revision goes into the publication.

Also, for stories that don't require immediate publication (a feature story, for instance), you will be expected to write the story in much the same way that a fiction writer does—long enough to fully tell the story, but short enough to hold the reader's interest.

In other words, your revisions of the story can focus entirely on the story's actual merits, not on how its length fits into a design on a page.

Freelancing On-line

For a variety of reasons, many newspapers are using more freelancers now than they have in past years, not only for travel stories and for covering high-school sports (two traditional spots to freelance for a newspaper), but also on the regular feature page and in suburban editions of the paper.

Newspapers traditionally use code words in the byline to denote that a story was written by a freelancer. Watch for the words "correspondent" or "special to the Daily News" to appear under the writer's byline. Those terms usually mean the story was written by a nonstaffer.

For the freelancer, the new technologies are perfect for newspaper work. Using your computer and a modem, you can do much of your research, including the occasional e-mail interview, then write the story, revise it, and send it directly into the newspaper's computer, where your editor can bring it up on her or his screen and begin the editing process.

All of this can quite easily take place without the story ever having been in hard copy until the day it appears in the newspaper.

The situation is a bit different for magazine work, where there is often a huge stack of unsolicited manuscripts and queries, the deadlines are rarely as pressing as those for a newspaper, and the space limitations were already typically easier than those for a newspaper even in precomputer days.

Even with their on-line versions, most magazines will continue to have regularly scheduled editions once a week, a month, or perhaps quarterly. Unlike newspapers, then, magazines will rarely think of themselves as 24-hour publications.

For the staffer, this means your deadlines will probably be about the same whether for a traditionally printed publication or for an on-line version.

The amount of space, though, may change dramatically. Because the number of pages of the on-line version is not tied directly to advertising (as it is with the regular printed edition), your stories can be as long as your editor thinks they need to be. This means the tightening-up aspects of revision (see Chapter 1) will be done purely to improve the story, not for reasons of space. It also means that the lengthening aspects of revision, where, for instance, the story gets longer as you add pertinent details or anecdotes to it, will become increasingly common.

Readability is an important part of an on-line publication's success. Large, easy-to-read type is important when you are looking at a publication on-line. This means that relatively few words fit on a given "page" of the publication, and, as many readers may be browsing through the on-line version looking for stories that interest them, it is quite possible that you will need to be able to write one very condensed version of the story that can be read in just one screen, and then a longer, complete version for the reader who wants more.

That first, condensed version will be much shorter than anything that might have appeared in the print version of the magazine. The longer, complete version is likely to be much longer than anything that might have been in the print version.

What You Can Expect

For the routine process of query letters and/or manuscript submission, there is not a lot of dramatic change. Editors simply are not ready yet to deal with thousands of submissions and queries by computer. For most editors, it is still much easier to work with hard-copy submissions and queries than with e-mail and electronic submissions, though that is beginning to change.

But once you have sold the idea or the manuscript, everything changes.

In the immediate future, what you can expect from the new technologies is a blend of things that greatly speeds up the process once you have sold a story and are into the revision work with your editor (as described in Chapter 7).

Because of the speed with which you can communicate with editors these days, you can expect to be working by fax and by modem rather than through the mail.

Let's take a look at a few examples of how this will work for you once you have the story under contract.

For an essay on elementary education for *World & I* magazine, I was contacted by the editor in charge of that section of the magazine, Lloyd Eby, and we agreed on the basic terms. He then sent a contract, which I signed. At that point we left the realm of what the computer hackers call "snail mail" (that is, the postal service), and moved into the much quicker mode of the facsimile machine, or faxing.

When I had the manuscript ready, it was very close to deadline, so I faxed it to Eby, and backed that up with a hard copy in the mail, along with a disk with the story in both ASCII (basic DOS text) and in WordPerfect (one of my favorite word processing programs).

Eby read and did his first edits on the story from my faxed copy, and so was ready to put the story into the magazine's computer and make his editing changes a few days later when the disk and hard copy arrived.

A day or two after that, he printed out the typeset version of the story as it would appear in print in the magazine, and faxed that to me so I could see his editing and respond to it.

Within 24 hours I had read the proofs, OK'd the changes (happily they were all quite minor), and faxed my comments back to Eby. The story appeared in print a few months later.

With a travel story for a local newspaper, we took the very large next step and skipped the hard copy phase entirely.

I had written several travel stories for this editor before, and she trusted me (see Chapter 7 for a reminder of how important this trust can be to your career).

We talked on the phone and agreed on the basic idea of the story, even talking about just what sidebars (those small stories that run alongside the main story) might be done, and what particular details of the trip I would touch upon.

A week or so later, when I finished my final draft of the story, I converted it from WordPerfect to ASCII in my computer, and used my modem software program to send it to the newspaper's computer directly through the phone lines.

In moments, my story traveled from my home computer to the newspaper's main computer, where the editor called it up on her screen and confirmed it had arrived.

That first draft was too long for her, though. She would have a tough time fitting it in, and asked me to cut. Because I had a day or two to work on it (in part because I could instantly send and receive comments and suggestions on the story through the modem connection), I decided instead to come up with a completely new, and shorter, draft of the piece, one I knew would fit the available space.

That new draft took a few hours to finish, and I sent it to the newspaper within five minutes of its completion.

The story ran in the paper a few days later, and its appearance in the paper was the first time that particular story had been in any hard copy at all.

Here's another example. As the editor of the newspaper's unusual short-story supplement, occasionally I solicit stories from writers and have them send me their drafts via e-mail through one of the on-line services or through a direct computer-to-computer link.

Frequently I receive the story, read it, have some thoughts on revisions, send the story back to the writer with a request for the revisions, and then wait a few days to get the piece back once again. After two or three of these electronic editing sessions, the story is usually ready for publication.

Finally, like a lot of writers, I sometimes collaborate on stories with other writers. We have found it very simple and effective to work on these collaborations through electronic editing sessions, sending various versions of the stories back and forth by computer until we reach a final draft that we think is ready for print.

Often, the editor to whom we send a given story then has some of his or her own ideas on revisions, and so a three-way transfer begins. Ultimately, the story is ready and appears in print.

It is entirely possible that this kind of electronically based writing will soon appear only in the electronic Internet or on-line service version of the magazine or newspaper. When that happens, the story will *never* have appeared in hard copy at any point in its existence.

For some publications, that is exactly what is happening right now. The wise writer is prepared for this, and comfortable with the computer hardware and software that is necessary for all this to happen.

Is this the way things will work for you? The answer is yes, almost certainly, and sooner than you may think.

The principal change in terms of editing and revision is that you will be able to work with an editor much more rapidly, and much more closely, than you could before. The overall quality of the story, and the speed with which it gets into print, should improve as a result.

Some On-line Terms

To be able to take advantage of the new technologies, you will need to have a computer, a modem, and the right software, and be comfortable using them. You will also need to know some computer terms. To help with that, here is a glossary of just a few of the terms that you need to know.

> *bulletin board:* An electronic gathering spot for a group of people with similar interests. Members can post messages to each other about any given topic.

CD-ROM: Compact disk, read only memory. A compact disk that offers words, visuals, sound and action, search capabilities, and more. Can only be read by the user, with no opportunity to write to the disk. Requires a CD-ROM drive in your computer.

desktop publishing: A software and hardware package that allows you to design, write for, edit, and produce a publication entirely on-screen with your computer. Two of the most popular software packages for this are PageMaker and QuarkXpress.

facsimile (fax):   An electronic method of transmitting pictures and text over telephone lines. Can be stand-alone machines or software packages in your computer. If in your computer, many fax software programs include a built-in scanner, to convert an incoming fax to text rather than receiving it as an image only.

hard drive: The drive unit in your computer where the memory is located and files are stored.

home page: A site on the Internet where an electronic publication exists.

information superhighway: A nickname for the Internet and other associated on-line services and research tools.

Internet: A global network of computer networks that allow instant access to home sites, bulletin boards, and much more.

Lexis/Nexis: Research tools that hold the electronic text versions of thousands of newspapers, magazines, law reviews, court decisions, and more.

on-line services: Electronic services that, for a fee, allow the user access to a wide variety of electronic services, usually including Internet access.

search engines: A search tool that allows you to find home sites and bulletin boards and more on the Internet. Among the most popular are Yahoo, Web Crawler, Gopher, Archie.

software: Electronic packages that allow you to perform tasks with your hard drive. Two common word processing software packages, for instance, are Word and WordPerfect.

sysop: Systems operator. The person (or persons) who runs and supervises a bulletin board.

telecommuting: Working by computer and modem from home, connected to the office by phone lines.

teleconferencing: Conferencing by phone lines and/or computer links.

URL: Uniform Resource Locator. The "address" of your site on the web.

World Wide Web: A tool that links files and sites on the Internet, allowing you to jump instantly from one site to another.

word processing: Special software packages that allow you to write, edit, and manipulate copy in your computer.

Exercises

1. If you have a home computer and a modem, one of the first things you need to learn is how to send stories via modem. To do this, arrange with another writer for the two of you to send complete copies of stories back and forth to each other. You will have to learn the limits and capabilities of your own hardware and software, but when you do you should be able to at least send ASCII versions of your stories back and forth.

2. If you have a computer and a modem, find your way onto the Internet and see if your local newspaper has a presence there. Next, find the on-line version of a major newsmagazine. Compare the two on-line publications. Describe what kind of on-line publication you would create if given the opportunity.

3. What do you think newspapers and magazines will look like in 5 years? In 10? In 20? Write a few paragraphs describing your local daily newspaper as it currently exists, and then a few more paragraphs describing how that paper might look in 5, 10, and 20 years. Do the same exercise with your current favorite magazine.

CHAPTER

10

Legal Matters

Legal issues and ethical standards should be major areas of concern for any staff writer or freelancer, and some legal and ethical matters touch directly upon the editing and revision process. Just how far can an editor go, for instance, in changing your copy if you are a staff writer or if you are a freelancer? What are the legal limits? The ethical limits? Who is responsible if an editor changes your copy and then there is a problem with copyright or libel law?

This chapter deals with those issues and also offers a basic primer in the ethics of editing and revision, libel law for staff writers and freelancers, and basic copyright law. This is material you need to know as you build your career in newspaper, magazine, or public relations writing.

Ethics

Most editors will treat your story with respect, contacting you when revisions are necessary and working with you to get your revisions done, no matter what the contractual arrangement for the story.

Occasionally, though, an editor will make changes (sometimes substantial ones) without contacting you. That is especially common in the newspaper business, where deadline pressure sometimes makes it impossible to talk to the writer about changes.

Ethically and legally, the editor has the right to make those changes. In the case of staff writers, your work is considered "work for hire" under copyright law (see the list of terms and definitions at the end of this chapter for an explanation of "work for hire"), which means the publication has paid you to write the copy and now the publication owns it entirely. The editor, therefore, can make any changes he or she finds necessary before putting the story into print.

The same standards apply, for the most part, to freelance material, though in this case it is not "work for hire," it is usually "first North American serial rights" (again, see the terms and definitions at chapter's end), which give the publication the right to use (and edit) the story for one-time use, after which the rights revert to you.

Freelancers usually find themselves signing a contract that sets out the legal issues for the writer, but those contracts rarely deal with the issue of editing and revision. A few court cases have addressed the question, but the result of those cases is muddled. For now, assume that the editor has the legal right to edit your copy.

At best, you can include a clause in your contract that stipulates that if the revisions or editing are unacceptable to you, you can have your name removed from the story so it is not under your byline.

As we discussed in Chapter 7, though, having the *right* to edit your copy without discussing the changes with you doesn't mean the editor *should* do that. Instead, the normal practice is for the editor to work with you on changes. Theoretically, you and your editor both have the same goal in mind, which is to make your story the best it can be when it appears in print.

The late Murray Cox, senior editor at *Omni* magazine for many years, thought the editor's role is to be the writer's "handmaiden," working with the writer to maximize a story's potential, making it the very best story it can be.

For Cox, as for most editors, it was important that the story remain the writer's as much as possible.

Cox's standard practice was to send along a several-page comment sheet to the writer, talking about the revisions that Cox had in mind for the story. This sheet, together with the marked-up copyedited version of the story (the copyedited version dealt mainly with grammar and style problems), was sent to the author, and then the phone calls started between Cox and the writer.

Eventually, a strong, polished story emerged, one that pleased both Cox and the writer, and one that was still very much in the words of the writer.

Not all editors are like Cox, of course. "I've worked with rewrite editors who can be very cavalier," he said. "They sometimes turn articles so far upside down that, well, writers have a legitimate gripe with those kinds of editors. I have seen articles that go into print and you could look through and maybe identify ten sentences that were really the writer's. Something's wrong there when that happens."

From the writer's perspective, it can be frustrating to do the research, the writing, and the revisions on a story, have the magazine accept it, and then see it changed dramatically when it appears in print.

The ethical standards of the field do allow for this to happen, especially under deadline pressure, but it certainly is not a happy occurrence for the writer, even for the beginner who is otherwise thrilled just to see the story in print.

Still, it's all part of the learning process for writers. If this kind of editing should happen to you, calm down and take a look at what has been done to the story. In most cases the editor will have improved the piece, and once you can admit that, you will be able to go through and see just how the improvements were made. Talk to the editor about the changes, if you can, and then try to turn in a story to that editor the next time that doesn't need, or get, as much editing.

If the editor has made changes that alter the meaning of the story or otherwise have a negative impact on you as the writer (invented quotes, for instance, or the deletion of a crucial passage that affects the meaning of a later passage), then the ethical line may have been crossed and you have a reason to complain. Make clear to the editor that what appeared in print was not what you wrote in the draft that you sent to the publication, and, if necessary, ask for a retraction or apology in the next issue of the publication.

But, a word of warning. It is easy for writers to be far too sensitive in these matters and to think the issue at hand is substantial when it is really quite small. Make sure you calm down and take a reasoned look at the changes before you harm your relationship with that editor by calling or firing off a heated letter of complaint that you may later regret.

If something like this comes up with your writing, have a mentor take a look at it from a fresh, nonbiased perspective. Only if that mentor upholds your feelings about the piece should you even consider contacting the editor about it.

Libel

Libel is written defamation of someone in print. Libel causes injury to a person's reputation, and you need to be cautious about putting such things into print.

However, there are sometimes cases in which something defamatory is exactly what needs to be said. The important thing then becomes, do you have a defense for a charge of libel? That is, if the case should go to court, who will win?

In the United States, the first principle in defending a libel suit is that the truth is the great defense. The tradition of truth as the great defense goes all the way back to colonial days, and if what you have said is provably true, you should be protected. Remember that what you say must be *provably* true, which means the burden of evidence is on you. Hang onto your notes, including research and interviews, to be on the safe side.

The other major element to libel law in the United States revolves around privilege. Privilege begins with government officials, who have what is called absolute privilege. In our free and democratic society, government officials in the performance of their duties are free to say what they choose to, and cannot be successfully sued for libel for those statements. This privilege starts with the executive, legislative, and judicial branches of the federal government and works its way all the way down to your local city council and its meetings.

Writers who cover the news generated by those officials are protected by what is called qualified privilege, a watered-down version. You are free to write about what these officials say, but be wary, your protection is not as complete as theirs. They can wander freely in their discussion, but you, generally speaking, need to stay close to the issue at hand.

Note that these qualifications vary from state to state, and you should know the libel standards in your state if you are doing a piece on government officials.

The third major component of libel law in the United States revolves around public figures.

Starting with the U.S. Supreme Court's decision in *N.Y. Times v Sullivan*, the high court has consistently upheld a writer's right to talk about a public official's performance as long as the story is not "malicious." In the Sullivan case, the high court defined malice as running a story when you have "knowledge that it (the information) was false, or reckless disregard of whether it was false or not."

This decision, referred to by journalists as the New York Times Rule, has since been expanded from public officials to include all public figures who are willingly in the public's eye.

Subsequent court cases have expanded or contracted the *New York Times* Rule's level of protection for writers. Currently, we seem to be in a period of contraction (that is, less coverage), including some hints that the "malice" standard may be changing to one of "negligence," which is easier for writers to stumble over, because it doesn't seem to presuppose purposeful intent, as does malice.

Generally, though, there is still solid protection for you when you write about public figures, as long as your story pertains to their public personas.

When it comes to matters of editing and revision, you can certainly expect your editor to want to change material that he or she thinks could be libelous. It is the publication that will be sued for the libel, because it either hired you as a staffer and so owns your story as "work for hire" or it has bought the one-time use of the story under current copyright law. The editor's job is to protect the publication from being successfully sued for libel. Expect your editor, then, to be touchy about this topic.

However, you should also take a good look at your contract if the publication gives you one. There may be a clause in the contract that absolves the publication from any risk for libel or for copyright infringement—two persistent worries in the publishing business. When you sign that contract, you assume the risk for libel.

Most magazines, of course, have fact-checkers, who will double-check every detail in your story. In theory, by the time your piece gets into print you, your editor, and the fact-checkers will have thoroughly gone over the story several times to make sure it is accurate, fair, and truthful. You should be fully protected.

Newspapers don't have the time for fact-checking at that level, and so are especially touchy about anything that might be libelous. Typically, any story with libel potential will be shown to the paper's lawyers before the story gets into print.

Copyright

If you are, or plan to be, a staff writer for a newspaper or a magazine, copyright law will be very simple for you. All your work is owned by the publication and that's that. As "work for hire" for the publication, you have given up the rights to the material through your contract to work for the publication.

This doesn't mean that you won't be able to reprint the article elsewhere, but it *does* mean that you should get permission from the publication that owns your work before you even send the piece out for consideration elsewhere.

Contracts vary, but most newspapers and magazines have clear rules about their staffers doing freelancing. For most newspapers, freelancing is fine as long as you are not selling your work to a competitor in your readership area. For magazines, similarly, outside writing is often fine as long as you are not selling to a competitor.

For freelancers, the situation is a bit more complicated. When you are freelancing you are usually, in effect, selling a publication the right to use your story once, after which the rights to the story revert back to you.

Selling Literary Rights

There are several basic kinds of rights that you can sell to a publication:

First Serial Rights

To sell *first serial rights* (or *first North American serial rights*, which includes Canada) means that you have sold the publication the rights to your story for one-time publication. After that one publication, the rights automatically revert back to you. This is the most typical situation for a freelancer, and is considered the industry standard, though many publications may alter it or vary from it by contract.

Second Serial Rights

To sell *second serial rights* (sometimes called "reprint rights") means that you are giving a publication the right to reprint *once* a story of yours that has already appeared in print elsewhere. After that second appearance, the rights again revert back to you for subsequent sales.

You can expect to receive less for a story when these reprint rights have been bought, but that's part of the appeal for both writer and editor. From the editor's perspective, if the story didn't appear the first time in a publication where many of his or her readers were likely to see it, this is an inexpensive way to get a good story into print.

From the writer's perspective, even if the second appearance pays less, that's better than nothing at all if the story is simply left in a drawer or on a hard drive, which is what happens to most stories after they are in print the first time. And, of course, a reprint doesn't usually require any real effort.

All Rights

Some publications buy *all rights* to your story, which means that the publication, not you, holds the copyright thereafter. If the publication has sister publications that might use the story later, or publishes books that use stories from the magazine, then this makes sense for the editor.

You want to be very wary of selling all rights, because the story is no longer yours once you have done so. However, a publication that buys all rights normally pays a much higher fee for the story than it would just buying one-time rights, and you may feel, under some circumstances, that the higher fee outweighs the loss of the story.

Work for Hire

In a *work for hire* situation, the publication or firm has hired you to write something, and that material thereafter belongs entirely to the publication or firm. Staff writers for newspapers or magazines normally work under a work for hire system, which means that the stories they write belong to the publication, not to the writer.

Public relations writers, whether working for a company or for a public relations firm, most typically are under a work for hire agreement, as well.

For the great majority of staffers, the benefits of a steady paycheck, a health plan, and a regular place to publish their work far outweigh the fact that all the material written belongs to the publication or the firm and not to the writer.

Fair Use

Fair use is a term used in the Copyright Act of 1976 that states that the use of copyrighted work for "purposes such as criticism, comments, news reporting, teaching (including multiple copies for classroom use), scholarship, or research, is not an infringement of copyright."

Fair use takes into account whether or not the copyrighted work or excerpt of a work is being used by another writer for that writer's financial gain. If there is financial gain, then permission needs to be obtained. If there is no gain (in a classroom setting, for instance), then permission probably does not need to be obtained.

The amount of work being used is also a factor. This is a gray area. A few paragraphs from a short story will probably be all right, but a few lines from a short poem are probably not all right to use without permission.

The financial impact on the writer of the copyrighted work is clearly the most important aspect of the fair use standard. If you plan to use someone else's material for your own gain, get permission.

How to Copyright Your Work

How do you go about copyrighting your stories? It's simple. Do nothing. The 1989 revision of the Copyright Act of 1976 protects your work from the moment you have created it, so it is not necessary for you to fill in the copyright forms, pay the $20 registration fee, and send it all in to the copyright office. Protection is automatic when you create the story.

But, and this is an important warning, while it is not legally *necessary* to file for your copyright with the copyright office, it may be a good idea to do so when you think there may be later challenges to your work.

Such challenges are very rare, but if someone attempts to claim your work as his or hers, your having filed earlier will be an important factor in proving who did the work.

If you want to file for copyright, write to the Copyright Office, Library of Congress, Washington, DC 20559, or call 202-707-9100 and voice mail will take you through a process that will get the proper forms mailed to you. You will probably want to ask for Package 109.

An alternative, one not as legally protective as filing for copyright but one that should help if there is a dispute, is to mail your hard copy of your story to yourself by registered mail. Seal the envelope containing the story (and have a notary sign and stamp it for another layer of protection) and then send it to yourself by registered mail. The date is marked by the post office on registered mail, and if the envelope was firmly sealed and that seal is unbroken, that is evidence of when you first printed out the story.

You cannot copyright an idea, you can only copyright your expression of that idea through the words you use. Similarly, titles cannot be copyrighted, nor can facts. You can only copyright your words that express the facts and ideas.

Exercises

1. You turned in a story about your college's new student body president to the school paper, and the piece appeared in today's edition. Without asking you, the editors at the paper changed the story, including cutting several quotes that you thought important. Discuss how you handle this issue with the editors at the paper. What if facts were changed? What if quotes were added, rather than edited out?

2. Using the phone number listed in the text, call the Copyright Office and ask for the forms necessary to copyright your most recently completed article. Keep track of the time it takes for the forms to arrive.

11

Marketing Your Writing

If you want to be a successful freelancer, one of the first things you have to learn is how to market your work. The marketing of your stories is at least as important as the hard work of writing and revising them.

To be successful at marketing your writing for magazines and newspapers, you need to become adept at writing solid query letters and cover letters, you need to develop a good tracking system for your stories and for your income and expenses as a writer, and you need to become aware of the other kinds of freelancing opportunities for writers outside of the magazine and newspaper field. For a variety of reasons, you also should be aware of issues of sensitivity.

Query and Cover Letters

A *query letter* is the brief proposal that you send to an editor to see if he or she is interested in taking a look at your story. A *cover letter* is the brief letter that accompanies your manuscript when you submit it to an editor. Query and cover letters are both very important to your freelance career, and both need to be edited and revised just as closely as the manuscript itself.

One of the major tricks to writing effective query and cover letters lies in the art of brevity, and that is where you can help yourself through revision. Concise writing is a real necessity when you are trying in the space of one or two pages, to convince an editor to take a look at your story.

To remind yourself of some of the kinds of tightening you can do inside sentences, take a look at Chapter 7. Such things as getting rid of extra words and watching out for unnecessary jargon or redundancies are crucial in the query, where you are not only explaining your idea and offering your credentials, but also displaying your writing skills. If you have writing problems in your query letter, the editor is likely to think that you will have them in your final manuscript, too, and may reject your query for that reason alone.

The Query Letter

In the query letter, you need to clearly, quickly, and concisely explain your idea and discuss how it will work for that editor's magazine. You should also discuss briefly your credentials for writing the piece. Exhibit 11.1 gives an example of a one-page query letter.

You should try to keep your query letters as short as you can, but a two-page letter won't seem unreasonable to most editors if you have something worth saying. Exhibit 11.2 provides an example of a query that runs to two pages.

You can see that both of these queries accomplish the basics. They clearly explain what the idea is and they reassure the editor that the writer who wrote the query is the right one for the story.

The second query goes into considerably more detail, which helps the editor see the precise focus of the piece and how much research the writer has already done. In other words, the editor can feel reasonably confident that the second story will turn out to be the one the writer promised.

If you have done the research and can be that specific in a query letter, it is probably a good idea to do so. It worked for this particular query letter, which resulted in a contract from the magazine editor.

E X H I B I T   1 1 . 1

Sample One-Page Query Letter

January 20, 1996

Art Fellow
Editor in Chief
SmartArt Magazine
1234 Frame Street
Washington, DC 12345

Dear Art Fellow,

Robert Rock is one of the preeminent artists of our time, a maker of images so persuasive that his technique of layered photographic images has influenced every area of our visual culture.

I have a rare opportunity to interview Rock later this month when he visits the Nevada State campus where many of his early works are stored.

Rock has agreed to spend the afternoon looking over those early works while we conduct the interview. I think this will make a terrific story, one that adds to our understanding of this influential artist and his early work and gives your readers an unusual look at the rarely interviewed Robert Rock.

My credentials include frequent artist profiles for our local daily newspaper, the *Daily Gamble,* and a recent profile on folk musician Billie Sue, published in *Seventeen* magazine.

Thank you for considering the idea. I look forward to hearing from you.

Sincerely,

Ann Righter
1234 Blackjack Ave.
Gamble, Nevada 12234

EXHIBIT 11.2

Sample Two-Page Query Letter

September 17, 1995

Joan Editor
Editor in Chief
Traveling College Magazine
1234 State Street
Santa Catalina, Calif. 93105

Dear Joan Editor,

Every summer I lead a travel-study group to Ireland and Scotland. For this year's trip we spent most of our time in County Kerry, and several days, in particular, on the Dingle Peninsula, where I got my first good look at the Blasket Islands.

Just off the coast from Dunquin, the Blaskets were the literary rage of the early part of this century. The literary flowering began with a visit from J. M. Synge in 1905, who came to study the Irish language from native speakers, and escalated rapidly following his published accounts of the islanders. Synge's Pegeen Mike in *The Playboy of the Western World*, by the way, is based on his hostess during that first stay in the Blaskets.

Within a few years Yeats and Joyce, among many others, were referring to the islands in their writing, and scholars such as Norwegian Carl Marstrander and his student, Englishman Robin Flower, came to study the pure form of Gaelic spoken there.

By 1917 one of the better storytellers on the island, Tomas O'Crohan, began a book, *The Islandman*, that recounted his life on the Blaskets. The book appeared in 1928 and was an instant critical and commercial success. Other books by O'Crohan and other islanders followed, including Peig Sayer's *Peig*.

In all, there have been some 70 books either about the islands or written by the islanders, and there are, I suspect, more books still to come.

Changes in the fishing industry and easier access to the mainland eventually brought the population of the Blaskets so low that in 1953 the islands were abandoned, the final two dozen islanders moving to the mainland. Something very reflective of this is found in the recent film, *The Secret of Roan Inish.* It was a poignant end to the Blaskets and their literary awakening.

Why was there such literary interest in the Blasket Islands? That's the story I'd like to write for *Traveling College Magazine.* The answer lies partly in the renewed interest in Gaelic that began around the turn of the century, partly in the stark but full life the islanders led and their wonderful capacity to describe it. And part of the literary world's interest, I suspect, was simply a fad, sparked by Synge and Yeats, fanned by Flowers, and then in full flame as the islanders themselves found their way into print.

I will be back in that part of Ireland in a few months, and plan to visit the islands with two friends of mine who are native Irish speakers from Kerry. I'd like to write a piece that is descriptive of the people and the place, certainly, but one that also takes on the interesting and complex literary history of the place.

My credentials include dozens of travel stories for magazines and newspapers, some fifty published short stories (several of them nominees for major awards), another fifty published poems, about one thousand newspaper and magazine feature articles, and half-a-dozen books either published or under contract, including a new series of young adult sports mysteries and two new textbooks on writing and editing. I am on the journalism faculty at the University of South Florida, and edit the *Tampa Tribune*'s short-story supplement, *Fiction Quarterly.*

Thanks for considering the idea. I look forward to hearing from you.

Best,

Rick Wilber
1234 Beach Street
Beachville, Mass. 22222
(phone) 000.555.1212

Here are some hints on how to write, edit and revise your query letters to maximize their potential:

Do Your Research
There are two basic kinds of research that you need to do *before* you send in a query letter. The first is the research for the story. The more research you have done, the stronger your query is likely to be.

The second is the necessary research about your market for the story. Before sending a query letter off to a publication, you should at the very least have read about the publication in a good market guide. Better still, you should have read several issues of the publication and be confident that it does, indeed, use the kind of story that you are proposing. This will also allow you to check the magazine's masthead to make sure that there has not been a change in editors since your market guide was published.

Also, you should research the past contents of the magazine you would like to sell to and see if the magazine used a similar story within the past couple of years. If the magazine did use such a story, it is unlikely to use another, unless you are offering a fresh, new angle.

Look and Sound Professional
Remember this is your first time to communicate with the editor, so you certainly want to have your work look its best. Make absolutely sure there are no misspellings, no typos, no dangling participles, no capitalization problems, and so on.

The query is usually just one page long, sometimes two, rarely longer. There is simply no excuse for any sloppy mistakes.

Offer a Fresh Idea or a Fresh Angle on an Old Idea
This ties in with your research. Editors are always looking for a fresh idea, something that makes sense for them that they have not used before. If your idea is a fresh one, your chances of interesting the editor improve measurably.

If your idea is not a fresh one (let's say it's an interview with a famous athlete), then make sure it offers a fresh angle on this old idea. If you are going on a long canoe trip with a famous pro football quarterback, for instance, that story will have a better chance of success than a typical stadium interview before or after a game or practice.

List Your Credentials, Including Your Non-writing Credentials

It is understandable that editors would be more interested in a query letter from an established writer. If you have sold before, you are, in the eyes of the editor, more likely to be able to produce the kind of work the editor needs. If you are a beginner, you have not yet proven yourself and the editor will have to factor that beginner status into his or her decision.

It is important to remember that frequently your credentials outside of your writing career can help you sell a story. If you were a competitive ice skater in your youth, and your idea is for an interview with an Ice Capades star, for instance, your background is a significant credential that adds to the likelihood of your selling the story, so mention it.

The Cover Letter

A cover letter accompanies the completed manuscript. A solid cover letter should briefly explain what is contained in the manuscript,and also briefly list your credentials to write the piece. Exhibit 11.3 is an example of a cover letter.

You can see the cover letter is meant to simply give the editor a quick idea of what the manuscript is about, and then establish the writer's credentials.

Some words of warning: Don't try to make the cover letter tell too much about what's in the story. Let the story speak for itself. Also, don't threaten, bluster, or get too cute with your query letter or your cover letter. Remember that you are in competition with perhaps dozens of other query letters and manuscripts that have reached the editor's desk about the same time as yours. If your approach isn't polite and professional, you have little chance of success.

A final important consideration for queries and cover letters is to always include a self-addressed, stamped envelope (SASE).

Sample Cover Letter

September 17, 1995

Joan Editor
Editor in Chief
Traveling College Magazine
1234 State Street
Santa Catalina, Calif. 93105

Dear Joan Editor,

Every summer I lead a travel-study group to Ireland and Scotland. For this year's trip we spent most of our time in County Kerry, and several days on the Dingle Peninsula, where I got my first good look at the Blasket Islands.

The enclosed story talks about how the Blaskets were the literary rage of the early part of this century, with some two dozen books written by the islanders and dozens of other books written about them. In 1952 the islands were abandoned.

The story seems to me to be a good fit for *Traveling College* magazine. I hope you agree.

My credentials include dozens of travel stories for magazines and newspapers, some fifty published short stories (several of them nominees for major awards), another fifty published poems, about one thousand newspaper and magazine feature articles, and half-a-dozen books either published or under contract, including a new series of young adult sports mysteries and two new textbooks on writing and editing. I am on the journalism faculty at the University of South Florida, and edit the *Tampa Tribune*'s short-story supplement, *Fiction Quarterly.*

Thank you for looking at the story, and I look forward to hearing from you.

Sincerely,

Rick Wilber
1234 Beach Street
Beachville, Mass. 22222
(phone) 000.555.1212

Beginners sometimes don't realize how important this little detail is.

Keeping Track

One of the more neglected aspects of freelancing is the task of keeping track of things, from where your recent manuscripts have been sent, to news about where you might send the next one.

Tracking Your Work

This process of keeping track of things becomes especially important to you as you do more and more revising, because you will likely be revising one or two older stories that came back in the mail, while also working on the second or third (or fifth) draft of a new story, while also getting into the planning and research stages for something newer still.

It can get confusing, but computer software has made the task somewhat easier, because you can slightly change the file name for various drafts of each story and save them all, with a clear indicator of which is which.

For instance, the first draft of this chapter might be called "Chap10," the second draft "Chap10a," and the third draft "Chap10b," and on down the line. If your software allows you to give each draft a longer, more specific name, all the better.

Why save all the earlier drafts? Primarily because it is possible that come draft three or four or the final draft, you will regret having gotten rid of something that was in the first or second draft, and if you have saved them you will still have that material.

Even in the final draft you may be deleting, right at the end, entire paragraphs that you now realize just don't belong. You can easily save those bits and pieces from all your drafts in one catch-all file, called something like "Chp10pts" (for Chapter 10 parts) or, again, something with a longer and more explicit name if your software allows it.

Tracking the Market

Another thing you may want to keep track of is the writers'
market. Buying one of the annual market guides is always a
good idea, but a wise freelancer is one who keeps up with
things a lot more often than once a year.

Several of the writers' magazines include market reports as
part of their monthly content, and you might want to sub-
scribe to one or two of them or at least buy an occasional issue
to get an update.

Also, there are organizations that are focused on one writing
genre or another. Joining one of those groups almost always
brings with the membership a subscription to a regularly
published market report.

There are organizations of this type for mystery writers,
romance writers, science fiction and fantasy writers, horror
writers, nonfiction writers and many more. See about joining
whichever one (or ones) suits your needs.

Many of these organizations are aimed at more established
writers, by the way, and so have minimum qualifications for
entry (three sales to a professional trade publication, for
instance). If that is the case for the group you are interested
in, see if there is a beginner's level of admission, frequently
called something like an "Associate Membership." The market
reports alone will probably be worth the price of joining, even
at the beginner's level.

Another way of staying in touch with changes in the mar-
ketplace is on one of the writing services offered by the on-line
services such as Prodigy, America Online (AOL), CompuServe,
GEnie, or others.

Getting Advice

On several on-line services there are bulletin boards where you
can talk to and occasionally receive advice from established
pros. Several of the services offer for-pay writing instruction,
too, and that may be well worth your while if the teacher is
a good one.

Finally, there are writing groups in almost every city in the
country. These groups range from extremely useful to utterly

worthless or even dangerous to you in terms of the help they can give you in your writing career. This is especially so in matters of editing and revision.

If the group has some members who are skilled in some portions of the editing and revision process (an English teacher, for instance, who could be trusted in matters of grammar), then by all means take advantage of the opportunity to have your work read by them and consider their advice as you go through your revisions.

If, however, the person reading and critiquing your manuscript has no background at all in writing, editing, or revision, by wary of their "help," which may be quite wrong.

There are groups in which some of the members have successfully sold fiction or nonfiction to professional publications. Remember, though, that having sold one, or even many, stories does not necessarily make one a useful editor for someone else's copy.

The best kind of help to get when you are beginning is the advice and editing that you will receive from a *mentor*, someone who is skilled in the editing and revision process and is willing to spend the time and energy it takes to help you polish your skills in the same process.

That mentor may be a current or past professor of yours, a friend or relative who is a professional writer or editor, or someone you stumble into in the writing group you have joined.

When you find a good mentor, work hard to learn what you can from that person. Later, when *you* are the polished professional, turn around and give someone else the same sort of mentoring that you once received. We all gain as a result.

Tax Deductions for Writers

The tax codes are changeable, so you will want to check each year to see what deductions are available to you as a writer. But there are some standard areas you should be aware of.

You should be able to deduct your writing-related phone calls (including fax and modem expenses). To help keep exact track of this, you may want to consider a separate telephone line for your writing-related work. The cost of that line should be deductible.

You should also be able to deduct your paper expenses for your computer printer, as well as other computer-related expenses that are directly related to your writing, including software (word processing programs, fax/modem programs, ink cartridges or ribbons for the printer, and the like). You should also be able to deduct your photocopying expenses.

Remember that if your computer was bought primarily for your writing, that cost (or a portion of it) may be deductible, as well. The same is true for a photocopier and a fax machine.

You should be able to deduct all your mail costs for your writing. Keep receipts from the post office or alternative mail delivery system. In addition, you should be able to deduct the costs of your envelopes or other packages.

Travel expenses, when you are traveling to research a story, should be deductible. If you are doing a travel story for a newspaper or magazine, at least a portion of the trip should be deductible. The portion may depend on how much of the trip was for personal enjoyment and how much was for business purposes.

Hint: You will have a much easier time convincing the IRS of the legitimacy of travel expense deductions if you have the published clip of the story that resulted from the trip.

Those portions of the expenses to maintain and operate your automobile that directly relate to your writing should also be deductible. The tax forms have a mileage formula that you will need to follow. Gasoline expenses that directly relate are deductible, too, so keep those receipts.

The cost for traveling to and attending seminars and workshops that are related to your writing should be deductible. Keep all receipts for tuition, travel, and so on, of course.

Similarly, the cost for membership in professional organizations should be deductible.

A word of caution: Remember in all cases to check any deductions you plan with a certified public accountant (the expenses for hiring that CPA are deductible).

Also, the tax code is particularly strict on "home office" deductions for writers (or for anyone else). You will probably have a difficult time using a home office as a deduction. If you plan to try for this deduction, talk to a tax expert first.

Other Freelance Markets

Remember that there are a number of freelance writing opportunities outside of writing for newspapers and magazines. Corporations, not-for-profits, and even public relations agencies often hire freelancers to write or edit brochures and other special publications such as annual reports.

Also, the burgeoning computer-based publication market is hiring regularly—full-time, part-time, freelance, and work-for-hire—to meet its rapidly growing demand for text and graphic material. Writers who are comfortable with the new technologies (see Chapter 8) are especially in demand for this kind of work. One interesting kind of writing, for instance, is for the CD-ROM market, which frequently uses freelancers.

Sensitivity Issues

Being sensitive to the needs and expectations of your readers is an integral part of the editing and revision process, whether you are moving around blocks and sections of your story, thinking through the implications of the new technologies, working on improving your voice and tone, or just making sure your formats are correct.

Sensitivity is important, and your editor knows it. From a simple marketing standpoint, it is a rare editor who uses a story that demeans or offends a part of his or her readership, so you need to be understanding of that and make sure your writing successfully deals with the issue.

Some of the issues of sensitivity in writing are obvious, others are more subtle. Here is a rundown of several significant issues in sensitivity.

Gender Issues with Pronouns

Many publications no longer use the "he, him, his," pronoun for both male and female references. A sentence such as "The typical student wants to buy his textbooks at a bargain price" seems to imply that the typical student is a male. This is not only inaccurate (because there are more female than male college students nationwide and at many individual colleges and universities), but unfair to women students. A better way to write that sentence is: "The typical student wants to buy his or her textbooks at a bargain price," which allows the pronouns to refer to males or females. Another common solution is to make the original noun a plural ("Typical students"), thus allowing for the gender neutral "their" pronoun. The sentence then would read: "Typical students want to buy their textbooks at a bargain price."

The "his or her" solution is not always well liked by editors, because it seems clumsy to some editors and writers. It is, however, becoming more common and may soon work its way into common usage.

The plural solution is favored by some, but doesn't always work in the sense of the story. If, for instance, the story has been following a singular pattern throughout, the sudden plural won't make sense. In that case, a proper noun ("Typical student Jane Doe," for instance) may provide a solution. The sentence, then, would read: "Typical student Jane Doe wants to buy her textbooks at a bargain price."

Gender Issues with Job Titles

Historically, a number of job titles seemed to indicate a particular gender. The great majority of those job titles have been changed to gender-neutral terms, which you should learn and use.

For instance, the sentence, "The fireman saved the boy's life," seems to indicate that the "fireman" is male. In an era in which many of the people fighting fires are women, a better term is "firefighter," which is now in common use. The sentence should read: "The firefighter saved the boy's life."

"Police officer" instead of "policeman," is another example, and there are many others. Watch out for these gender-loaded terms as you revise.

Also, a number of job positions that once were held predominantly by one gender or the other (secretarial and nursing positions held by women, for instance) are now routinely held by either gender. Be careful about your pronoun use when referring to these positions, because contemporary use usually carefully considers the possibility that a nurse, a kindergarten teacher, a secretary, a doctor, an airplane pilot, or anyone else could be male or female.

Ethnic and Disability Labels

Contemporary usage for ethnic groups primarily relies on what that group calls itself, though in many cases that situation is confused when the group itself has internal differences. Which term is appropriate in your story, "African-American" or "black," for instance? It's a judgment call, and you will have to rely on your editor for the appropriate choice. The same holds true for "Native American" or "Indian," though Native American seems to be the more common usage these days. In all cases, make sure that your final draft conforms to the style usage of the publication for which you are writing.

For disabilities, the term you should use is whatever term the group seems to find most acceptable, though, again, in many cases that terminology may be in flux. The new terminology that uses the word "challenged," though clumsy, is sometimes the preferred term. In many other cases, though, the historically common term remains in use. In still other cases, a newer term ("hearing impaired," for instance) is the preferred choice. Check with your editor.

Exercises

1. Along with the other writers in your class or writers' group, write a version of a query letter that might have worked for writer Jeannette Batz when she was working on her story on Attention Deficit Disorder. Trade those query letters and see which sounds most effective. Why is that one effective? How could you change your letter to be more effective?

2. Think through all the expenses you might have for writing a magazine piece on a local politician. Figure in driving expenses, telephone expenses, computer

expenses like paper and ink, and any other relevant expenses. What is your total? What kind of yearly expenses might you have, given the number of stories you want to write? Write a two-page description of the kinds of records you need in order to keep track of your writing expenses.

3. Talk to a local tax consultant about your writing and its expenses and *then* write a two-page description of your expected annual expenses and how you will keep track of them.

Appendix

Sample Draft
and Published
Pieces

APPENDIX

A

Final Draft:

"Boxer Steve Langley Is No Champion, But He Fights On Because . . . He Can Take A Pounding," by Greg Couch

The bleeding finally stops, and Steve Langley waits behind half a dozen boxers lined up at the cashier's chain-link window to collect their pay. Fifteen minutes earlier, he was leaning backward over a dirty sink in a dirty bathroom while three stitches were hurriedly sewn into his forehead to stop the blood that had been spurting straight up as if from a sprinkler.

The blood had stopped the fight 1-1/2 minutes into the second round, when Langley and world welterweight champion Maurice Blocker simultaneously threw jabs and accidentally butted heads on the follow-through. Although Langley had landed the only two solid punches, under the rules, the fight hadn't gone enough rounds for the judges to determine a winner. The ruling: technical draw.

"A draw? With the world champion?" the other boxers in line say to Langley. "People fight a lifetime for something like that. With a world champion? Twenty years from now you'll be telling people. You had a draw? With a ..."

139

It does serve as consolation. After all, how often does a machine worker from a Wichita plastics plant get a chance to fight a world champ? Much less fight him to a draw?

But Langley sees only a lost chance to prove himself.

And then, another blow, out of the ring, the kind that hurts Langley more in the hours and days after the fight than any of Blocker's punches.

As he's handed his pay, an amount he isn't willing to disclose "and don't forget the 200 for expenses" Langley's hit with the news that the decision has been changed after complaints from the champ's corner.

The new ruling: no contest. As if the whole thing never happened.

Before the fight, he had said that a guy like him would never get a fair shake against a champ.

Then the stomach churned. And the pressure grew. And the bell sounded. And the biggest fight in Steve Langley's life never happened.

"If this never happened," he says afterward, "I must not be here."

By 4:30 a.m. Wednesday, May 19, the day before the fight, Langley is on the driveway of cutman Pete Diaz of Wichita, getting ready for the 6-1/2-hour drive to Omaha. Just 2-1/2 days earlier, Langley had received a call asking whether he wanted to fight Blocker on Thursday in a non-title bout.

Typical for Langley, who is often treated as an afterthought.

At 32, he's a top-notch local, even a top regional, fighter. He held the 13-state Mid-America title belt at 154 pounds, the junior middleweight division. He gave up that belt when he pulled out of a scheduled title defense to fight Blocker.

"It's not that I'm any great thing," Langley says. "I've been beaten up by the best of them. I'll be honest, when I leave town, my chances of winning are slim and none. They choose you a guy in the top 10, he's got multimillion-dollar backers and he knows exactly how you fight before they pick you.

"I've got a real good chin; that's what I'm known for. That's it. Not that I can fight very good. Just that I can take a punch. You hit me all day, and I'm still there. That's what people say the first time they see me. 'By God, you can really take a beating.'"

As a top journeyman, Langley gives a champ or contender plenty of work before a big fight without being much of a threat to win.

He's a hired chin, fighting with a million-to-1 odds against him. And he'll take those odds.

A stop at McDonald's at 8:30 a.m., and Langley watches dryly while his passenger has Egg McMuffins, orange juice and coffee. Langley doesn't order anything.

"How's that coffee?" he asks with envy. "Oh my God, he's putting cream in there."

When Langley agreed to take the fight, he was told that if he weighed more than 154 pounds, the fight was off. He hopped on the scale, which read 168, and said to count him in.

For the next three days, he ate salads and vegetables and nothing to drink, thank you. By Tuesday evening after work, he was so weak and sluggish, he could spar just two rounds.

So McDonald's coffee tantalizes. With cream.

But the worst comes an hour and a half later, at the Squaw Creek Plaza truck stop in Mound City, Mo., where an awful machine asks, "How much do you weigh???"

Langley goes into the bathroom and puts on a black plastic sweat suit, hoping to pull out those last remaining drops of sweat. He buys a pack of gum and takes a Styrofoam cup to spit into until weigh-in so he won't swallow his saliva. Added weight, you know.

He jacks up the heat in the car full blast, and 20 minutes later takes his hand off the steering wheel and puts it down by his side. Sweat pours from his sleeve like water from a pitcher.

A long, flat road, little scenery, 4:30 in the morning, McDonald's to drool over the coffee with cream, a weight scale, plastic sweat suit and spit into a cup.

Ptt-fht.

Langley, of course, has no way of knowing that the champ, who had flown in, will miss weight by 4 pounds and the fight will go on. No big deal.

After all, he is the champ.

The sweat is still dripping when Langley starts telling war stories.

When he fought Darrin Van Horn, who had just lost his title, Langley went down with two broken ribs in the first round, then got up and finished the 10-round fight, losing by decision. Afterward, Langley went to Van Horn's locker room to thank him for the fight, and Van Horn had both hands in a bucket of ice.

"He says to me. 'What have you got in your head?' " Langley says. "I broke my ribs, but at least I got to say I broke both of his hands on my face."

Doubt his stories and he produces evidence. Supermiddleweight contender Tim Littles said Langley was the toughest fighter he had ever faced.

Yeah, sure.

And then, sure enough, he pulls out the February 1993 issue of World Boxing magazine, with an interview with Littles that backs up Langley's story.

And you realize he's not just telling tales. Especially when he insists that anyone telling his story should include the negatives.

"Just let it be truthful," he says. "Tell the bad stuff or people won't believe the good stuff. They'll just think I'm full of it."

Langley tells of the time he got into a heated argument with his wife, Ramona, that landed him in jail for a few hours. As a football player at Emporia High, he says, he used to sign up for classes that were taught by coaches, then have his grades improved for him. Because of that, for which he blames himself, he says he reads at a sixth-grade level. He has overcome a drinking problem that years ago saw him drunk during fights.

"I've grown up since then," he says.

He proved that when he turned down an offer from Lou Duva, manager of former heavyweight champ Evander Holyfield, to be a sparring partner at $500 a week. He didn't want to do without the medical benefits he gets at Pawnee Extrusions for his wife and 4-year-old son, Steven.

Langley likes to talk about Steven: "When he was a baby, I saw him grab the bars in his crib and start banging his head on them. I thought, 'Hey, he's going to make a good boxer.' "

And he talks about the early days of his marriage, when he lived in a six-man tent, then a trailer, then a small apartment. He bought his house on Wichita's south side soon after Steven was born, figuring a child needs a house.

Like his boxing, Langley's real life is a matter of taking a shot and then moving on.

He arrives in Omaha just before noon, two hours before the news conference, and his concern turns away from his light-headedness and dehydration.

"I hope the hotel has some big towels," he says. "We'll need them in the corner. We might return them with a little blood on them, though. Ha, ha, h a."

That nervous laugh.

He had demonstrated it over and over the entire drive, making at least a million jokes. Like when Diaz had complained that Langley kept driving on the shoulder.

"I'll be OK," Langley had said. "I might have a problem on the way back, though. I might not be able to see after my eyes are swollen shut."

He gets to the desk at the Embassy Suites hotel, and the promoter has forgotten to reserve a room for him.

Treatment for a world champ and treatment for Steve Langley will always be different. Eventually, though, the hotel finds him a room.

At 12:30, he's in shorts and a T-shirt on a scale in the deli in the hotel lobby. 156. Two more pounds.

Back to the plastic sweat suit, this time to sit on the edge of the tub while running the shower for steam.

At the news conference, Angelo Dundee, former trainer to Muhammad Ali, sits at the table next to the podium with his three young fighters. A former world cruiserweight champ is also at the table. And Blocker and his lawyer.

The rest of the boxers stand around the room and watch.

The fighters at the table are introduced, and then the ones around the room, all except Langley.

Ask Blocker a question. Get an answer from his lawyer, James Cooke. Cooke has a perfectly tailored $500 suit, perfect sparkling shoes, perfect haircut, perfect gold brace-let, perfect nails.

Why have Blocker fight Langley in Omaha?

Because, Cooke says, Blocker has a title fight next month and needs to get back into the ring. And Blocker is a Don King fighter and Don King stands for America and Nebraska is part of America . . .

Perfect.

Meanwhile, Langley looks to Diaz, the cutman in a blue windbreaker, jeans, tennis shoes and Wichita River Festival T-shirt, and tells him to register as a trainer because cutmen, who close fighters' cuts and stem bleeding, cost more to register.

"Oh, yeah, I almost forgot," the promoter says. "Also fighting is Steve Langley, standing over there, from Wichita, Kansas. He accepted at the last minute to fight a world champion and a lot of people wouldn't do that, so you have to give him credit for that, at least."

Later, Langley will admit that this kind of treatment bothers him.

The interviews end, and Langley asks Blocker for an autograph. Blocker obliges and thanks Langley for taking the fight. He couldn't get anyone else.

Time for the weigh-in and Langley strips down to his purple underwear and socks, creeps onto the scale, and . . . 154. He dresses and runs straight to the bathroom to drink from the faucet.

Blocker bothers only to take off his shoes. He weighs 158.

Fight day arrives, and Langley's feeling better. After the weigh-in, he had gone out for dinner: New York strip, double mashed potatoes, cup of coffee, a hamburger, french fries, two glasses of milk and a slice of lemon meringue pie. And breakfast on fight day is a cheese omelet, two glasses of milk and a bottle of Gatorade.

Oh yeah, Diaz remembers, they need scissors to cut the tape off the bottom of the gloves. So it's over to the mall, where they don't have the right kind, the ones with the flat nose.

"I could just pull the tape off with my hands like I usually do," Langley says. "Pete just wants to look important."

It takes three more stops to find the scissors before going back to the hotel.

Oh yeah, Diaz remembers, they need Vaseline. Back to the mall, where, at $3.29, Vaseline is too rich for Diaz's blood. Luckily, the store has its own brand for $1.79.

Langley has been in fast motion all day. Talking fast. Walking fast. Joking fast. Laughing fast. The nerves are building.

Meanwhile, in the deli in the lobby, Blocker's manager buys his fighter some pasta salad. What has Blocker been doing all day? Sleeping.

Langley becomes serious for the first time since accepting the fight.

"It's not that I'm scared . . . well, maybe it is a little scared," he says. "When I fought Van Horn, I let the bright lights get to me. That's not going to happen this time. When I fought Tim Littles, that was a nightmare, a nightmare come true. He just kept hitting me.

"Normally, a guy hits you and you see a sparkle and hear a hum. He'd hit me and I'd just see white. For three or four weeks after that I was thinking about it."

Langley's trainer, Tony Gallardo, shows up just before 6, minutes before the trip to the Coliseum. He made the drive after finishing his shift at Boeing. Hardly anyone is at the Coliseum when Langley checks in. Gallardo is given a name tag that reads "Tony Delgado."

"Close enough," Langley says.

Meantime, Cooke, Blocker's lawyer, enjoys a drink and some pretzels in the Coliseum lounge, talking about Blocker.

"He goes all over," says Cooke, in another perfect suit. "Next month, he'll fight in San Diego for the championship on Showtime. So it's bright lights, big city, fast cars . . ."

Potato chips and coffee. That's what one of the boxers is snacking on in the locker room before the fights. He's sitting calmly, not bothering to build a sweat in a roomful of nervous fighters.

"Something like that would make a boxer sick to his stomach," Langley says. "He must not be thinking it's going to be a very long fight."

Sure enough, the potato chip eater fights someone who introduced himself a day earlier as Kevin, but now, somehow, is fighting under the name of Jimmy McClain. The chip-eater knocks out McClain, or whoever he is, in the first round.

One of the fight's organizers takes Langley aside and tells him not to be a hero. If he starts to get hurt, he shouldn't let the fight go on.

Not Langley. He still dreams of being a hero. He puts his name on the line as well as his chin.

In the three hours before the fight, Langley gets last-second instructions from Gallardo — "move close to avoid his long arms" — goes to the bathroom, then to a corner to sit by himself. Instructions. Bathroom. Corner.

At last count, 12 trips to the bathroom.

"A lot of people just see this as a payday," he says. "I see it as an opportunity."

Once, Langley capitalized on the opportunity, beating a contender named Carlos Cruz. Langley has a poster from that fight on his living room wall, next to the stationary bike, a few feet from the picture of Rocky Marciano.

He sends someone to Blocker's locker room with a message:

"Tell him I'm not here to play. Tell him I'm here to fight."

In the ring and out, Langley's always moving in, leading with his head. He puts his face in front of you and says, "Go ahead, hit me." You throw a punch, he doesn't move, and "BOOM" right in the face. And he smiles, leans in with his head and dares you again.

He says he used to think that the sign of manhood was to take punches. His flat nose and puffy eyes are his badges.

At 10:44, he slips on the gloves. Langley, with shaved head and royal-blue shorts, is in the ring first. He waits for the champ, five minutes that seem like 50.

Finally, Blocker enters the ring in a fringed white robe and white shorts with an entourage of manager, cutman, lawyer and others.

At 10:52, PING!, the fight starts. Langley throws the first punch, a right cross that misses. Both fighters move slowly, the only pace Langley knows.

Blocker taps Langley with a soft six-punch combination. Langley smiles and moves in, landing a left jab to the jaw that backs Blocker up. He throws two wild hooks that miss, then a right cross that catches the champ on the chin.

The second round starts just as slowly, but then both throw jabs, heads collide, doctors run in, and at 10:58, it's all over.

Just 5-1/2 minutes after it started.

Langley runs to the center of the ring, hugs Blocker and tells him, "I'm sorry."

He climbs out of the ring and tells some guy in the front row, whom he doesn't know, that he's sorry. He tells some guys in the beer line on the way back to the locker room.

And in his own way, he tells Wichita.

"Do you think the people of Wichita should be proud to have me representing them?"

When he hears the decision is changed from technical draw to no contest, Langley can't believe it. He runs around asking people what they think the decision should have been.

"What you have there is a technical draw," Dundee says. "One of my fighters had that once."

But there was no changing it back. It was ruled by the head of the Nebraska boxing commission, Jesse Cardenas, who says that the rule book allows him to change the decision.

He asks why Langley cares so much.

"Blocker was just coasting, he wasn't putting no pressure on him," Cardenas says. "In another round, he would have started to put the pressure on.

"Would you think that if they stop the fight like that in the second round it should be called a draw? With a world champ? Langley's not even a ranked fighter. Now, if he were, I might look at it different."

At a postfight reception, Diaz keeps shushing Langley, failing to keep him from complaining to everyone.

"If he makes too big of a fuss," Diaz says, "he'll never be invited back. People aren't going to want him if they know he raises a fuss. That's just the way the game is played."

So this is where it ends. None of it ever happened. And Langley might not be invited back.

Blocker flies home to prepare for his title fight. He leaves with his belt intact, his record intact, his future intact.

It never happened.

By the next morning, the swelling under the stitches in Langley's head is starting to go down. He has 6-1/2 hours of flat, hot road ahead to get back to Wichita for the next day's work. And to wait for another chance.

(END)

Source: *Wichita Eagle*, June 7, 1993, with permission.

APPENDIX

B

First Draft:

"The Heart of Scottish History," by Sherry Long

For centuries, Edinburgh has been the heart of Scottish history. Edinburgh is a walking city. Pack a comfortable pair of tennis shoes, a light jacket and a strong sense of adventure and you will be prepared to experience a city full of charm, history and even a castle. You will be able to literally walk everywhere you need to go throughout this beautiful city. There are taxi's and buses available for those wanting to save tread on their shoes, but you can experience the cities flavor so much more when you walk its streets and byways. The people are very friendly and always seem glad to point out special sites or points of interest. If you get lost, you can always hail a cab and have them drop you at a familiar destination.

At the center of the city, sitting high atop an extinct volcano, is the most famous castle in the world...the Edinburgh Castle. The Edinburgh Castle was built on the site of an Iron Age fort. The castle can be seen from just about anywhere in Edinburgh. The castle's gray stone walls seem to be carved right out of the black stone it is perched on. The castle and its pedestal are lighted and offer a breathtaking view at night. The castle is open to the public and features several museums. The Crown Jewels of Scotland, the Great Hall (still used today) and an enormous 15th century gun: Mons Meg are some of the exhibits you will find within the walls of the great castle. The castle also has a full service restaurant that offers its dinners a magnificent view of the city while they dine.

Protecting the entrance of the castle you will find delightful Scottish guards. The guards are dressed in traditional Scottish kilts and they don't mind having their pictures made with visitors to the castle. The Edinburgh Castle sits at the top of High Street, a street known as the Royal Mile. A cobblestone street is full of shops, pubs and historical museums. Along the mile you will find St. Giles Cathedral, the 12th Century High Kirk of Edinburgh. This cathedral was the center of religious reformation and is open to the public. Inside the magnificent stone cathedral you will find a pipe organ dating back to the 12th century and a Thistle Chapel. Located a short distance from the cathedral is the historic Lady Stair's House built in 1622. Inside the house you will find the Writer's Museum. The museum is full of treasures relating to three of Scotland's most famous writers — Robert Burns, Sir Walter Scott and Robert Louis Stevenson. The Museum is open to the public and there is no admission charge.

The John Knox House is also located along the mile. This unique medieval house is a memorial to John Knox and was also the home of James Mossman, Mary Queen of Scots goldsmith. The Camera Obscura along the mile, offers an interesting view of Edinburgh from the top of its tower building. The Museum of Childhood located a few buildings down from the Camera Obscura, is a free museum that is home to toys and childhood memories. Along the mile are a multitude of shops offering traditional Scottish clothing, toys, treats and even bagpipes. I picked up a set of bagpipes for my son. The owner of the small shop played the pipes for me before he boxed them up for my return home. There are also plenty of small restaurants and pus to rest your feel while enjoying a scone and a cup of hot tea. During one of my ventures down the mile, I found an antique book store where I purchased a copy of Robert Louis Stevenson's book, Treasure Island. There are several books stores along the mile where you can pick up a book by one of Scotland's famous authors for just a few pounds.

At the end of the Royal Mile, east of the castle is the Queen of England's official Scottish residence - the Palace of Holyroodhouse. The palace was once home to Mary Queen of Scots, Prince Charles Edward Stuart and Bonnie Prince Charlie. The palace is open to the public except in July when it is home to the Queen and her family. Inside the palace you can tour the Throne Room, Royal Dinning Room, Morning Drawing Room and picture gallery housing more than 90 17th century portraits of Scottish monarchs. The palace is rich in neoclassic architecture and furnishings, and offer a glimpse into the world of royalty.

The palace is surrounded by an ornate iron wall with majestic iron lions perched high above the gates viewing the palaces' visitors. Sir Arthur's Seat offers a spectacular backdrop to the palace. Sir Arthur's Seat is an 820-foot volcanic remnant that sits in the center of Holyrood Park. The mountain looking rock is covered on one side with goarse, a prickly green shrub that has a brilliant gold flower perched atop its sharp leaves and trails leading to the top on the other side of the mound. Arthur's seat offers a challenging climb and a breathtaking view of Edinburgh, the Pentland Hills and the Firth of Forth that is well worth the climb. Holyrood Park is one of many parks in Edinburgh that is open to the public. North of the palace lies Edinburgh's historic port, Leith. Mary Queen of Scots landed at Leith on her return from France in 1561.

A short distance from the Royal Mile you will find Princess Street..a shoppers paradise. Princess Street is in the hart of Edinburgh's shopping district. Shoppers can enjoy hours of shopping at the many small shops and department stores located along this road. There are also many banks and restaurants if you need to refuel. As you make your way to Princess Street from the Royal Mile you may want to stop and visit the National Gallery. The

National Gallery has an outstanding collection of works by Rembrandt and Vincent Van Gogh.

Edinburgh has many restaurants and pubs that you can experience authentic Scottish dishes such as Haggis and fish and chips. I was surprised by the number of Italian restaurants I found in Edinburgh. One of my favorite restaurants was Bar Roma an Italian restaurant located several blocks off Princess Street. The restaurant was a lively place full of singing waiters, Italian memorabilia and Julia Roberts. Yes Julia Roberts was sitting by the desert counter on one of my visits to the restaurant. She was in town filming a movie and I was able to talk to her and get an autograph with the help of my comical waiter Bruno.

There is enough to see and do in Edinburgh to spend your whole time in Scotland there, but if you want to venture to other destinations, trains are available on a regular schedule and there are two train stations to serve you. Cramond, a small fishing village located a few miles from Edinburgh, can be reached by bus. It will cost you approximately 70 pence (about $1.00) to ride the bus to this enchanting little village with strong Robert Louis Stevenson ties. Cramond offers a slower more relaxed pace than Edinburgh. Along the Almond River located in Cramond, you can enjoy a leisurely walk along the rivers shore. Along your walk you can view the swans swimming against the tide or ducks walking along its wooded shore-line. The trail is covered by trees and lined by queen Anne's lace, daises and brilliant purple heather. Along the trail there is a dam and a rushing waterfall. There are also benches that you can rest your feet and take time to let your mind wander. Just offshore is Cramond Island. Cramond Island is the island that Robert Louis Stevenson played on as a child and later inspired him to write the book Treasure Island. The island can be reached by walking to it at low tide. There are signs warning that the bridge is covered by water at high tide. There are several small cafes and inns located in Cramond. The Cramond Inn was a favorite of Robert Louis Stevenson. The Cramond Cafe is a small quaint one room cafe featuring wonderful homemade desserts and soups. The 16th-century stone dining room has a large picture window that offers a stunning view of the harbor as you sip sweet warm chocolate. There are several small shops that you can purchase souvenirs of your visit. As you make your way back to the bus stop you will want to visit the remains of a Roman fort that dates back to the second-century. These remnants signify the furthest point that the Roman Empire went in Britain.

There are many hotels and bed and breakfast homes to stay in during your visit to Edinburgh. Bed and breakfast hotels offer a hearty home-cooked breakfast as well as a friendly atmosphere. You can obtain a list of Bed and breakfast hotels by writing or calling the Edinburgh and Scotland Information Centre, 3 Princess Street, Edinburgh Scotland. Phone 031-557-1700. The center will also be able to supply you with maps and brochures about Edinburgh and its wonderful sights.

A few tips while in Edinburgh:

- Invest in a lightweight all weather jacket. Scotland's weather can be unpredictable and light showers are a daily occurrence.
- Have plenty of change on hand when riding the bus. Bus drivers do not make change.
- Pack comfortable shoes and clothing. The weather can become quite chilly even in the middle of summer.
- Carry a card with your hotel address on it in case you get lost.
- Purchase a good map of the city listing its sights and points of interest. Some of the hotels supply their guest with complimentary maps and bro-chures.

Source: Sherry Long, with permission.

APPENDIX

C

Final Draft:

"The Heart of Scottish History," by Sherry Long

Edinburgh, Scotland's capital, is a wonderful city for walking. All that you need to see most everything in this compact and beautiful city full of charm, history and art is a comfortable pair of tennis shoes, a light jacket and a strong sense of adventure.

The people are very friendly and always seem glad to point out special sites or points of interest. If you get lost, you can always hail a cab and have it drop you at a familiar destination.

At the center of the city on an extinct volcano is Edinburgh Castle, one of the world's most famous. The castle can be seen from just about anywhere in the city, its gray stone walls seemingly carved right out of the black stone it is perched on.

Edinburgh Castle was built on the site of an Iron Age fort. The oldest part of the current structure, St. Margaret's Chapel, dates from the 11th century. The newest section of the castle and walls were added in the 17th century.

The castle and its pedestal are lighted at night and are breathtaking to view form the surrounding streets and parks.

The castle is open to the public and features several museums, the Crown Jewels of Scotland, the Great Hall (still used today) and an enormous 15th-century cannon, Mons Meg.

The castle also has a full-service restaurant that offers its diners a magnificent view of the city while they dine. Scottish guards, dressed in traditional kilts, protect the entrance to the castle and they don't mind having their picture taken with visitors.

The castle sits at the top of the Royal Mile, a cobblestone street full of shops, pubs and historical museums.

Along the mile you will find St. Giles Cathedral, the 12th-century High Kirk of Edinburgh. This cathedral was the center of religious reformation and is open to the public and still in use. Inside the charming stone cathedral you will find a pipe organ dating back to the 12th century.

Located a short distance from the cathedral is historic Lady Stair's House built in 1622. Inside the house is the Writer's Museum, full of treasures relating to three of Scotland's most famous writers - Robert Burns, Sir Walter Scott and Robert Louis Stevenson. The museum is open to the public and there is no admission charge.

The John Knox House is also located along the mile. This unusual medieval house was John Knox's home and was also the home of James Mossman, Mary Queen of Scots' goldsmith. The Camera Obscura at the top of the mile, offers an interesting view of Edinburgh from the top of its tower.

The Museum of Childhood located a few buildings down from the Camera Obscura, is a free museum that is home to toys and childhood memories. Also along the mile are a multitude of shops offering traditional Scottish clothing, toys, treats and even bagpipes.

I picked up a set of bagpipes for my son at one small shop. The owner played the pipes for me before he boxed them up for my return home.

During one of my ventures down the mile, I found an antiquarian book store where I purchased a copy of Robert Louis Stevenson's book, "Treasure Island." There are several antiquarian book stores along the mile.

At the bottom of the Royal Mile, east of the castle, is the Queen of England's official Scottish residence - the Palace of Holyroodhouse. The palace was once home to Mary Queen of Scot and Bonnie Prince Charlie.

The palace is open to the public and you can tour the Throne Room, Royal Dining Room, Morning Drawing Room and picture gallery housing more than 90 17th-century portraits of Scottish monarchs.

The palace is rich in neoclassic architecture and furnishings, and offers a glimpse into the world of royalty.

Surrounding the palace is an ornate iron wall with majestic iron lions perched at its gates. Arthur's Seat, an 820-foot volcanic remnant that sits in the center of Holyrood Park, offers a spectacular backdrop to the palace.

Gorse, a native Scottish shrub that has prickly green leaves and brilliant gold flowers, covers most of Arthur's Seat. Trails that snake around the mountain lead to its top where you will find a breathtaking view of Edinburgh, the Pentland Hills and the Firth of Forth.

North of the palace lies Edinburgh's historic port, Leith. Mary Queen of Scots landed at Leith on her return from France in 1561.

From the top of Arthur's Seat you can also see Princes Street, a shopper's paradise. Princes Street is in the heart of Edinburgh's shopping district. Shoppers can enjoy hours of shopping at the many small shops and department stores located along this road.

Edinburgh has many restaurants and pubs that you can experience authentic Scottish dishes such as haggis and fish and chips. I was excited to find Henderson's, a wonderful vegetarian restaurant that featured a buffet style fare at a reasonable price.

I was surprised by the number of Italian restaurants I found in Edinburgh. One of my favorite restaurants was Bar Roma, an Italian restaurant located several blocks from Princes Street.

The restaurant was a lively little place full of singing waiters, Italian memorabilia and Julia Roberts. Yes, Julia Roberts was sitting by the dessert counter on one of my visits to the restaurant.

Roberts was in town filming "Mary Reilly." The streets of Edinburgh's old town were a perfect backdrop for this 19th-century film.

With the help of my comical waiter, Bruno, I was able to talk to Roberts and get her autograph.

There are taxis and buses available for those wanting to save thread on their shoes, but you can experience the city's flavor so much more when you walk its streets and byways.

One city you can reach by bus is Cramond, a small fishing village located a few miles from Edinburgh. It will cost you approximately 70 pence (about $1.25) to ride the bus to this enchanting little village with strong Robert Louis Stevenson ties.

Cramond offers a slower and more relaxed pace than Edinburgh. You can enjoy a leisurely walk along the River Almond or the Firth of Forth shoreline.

As you walk you may encounter swans in the river swimming against the tide or ducks walking along its wooded banks. The trail is covered by trees and lined by Queen Anne's lace, daises and brilliant purple heather.

Along the trail there is a dam with a rushing waterfall. There are also benches located along the trail where you can rest your feet or just take time to let your mind wander.

Located just offshore from the river's mouth is Cramond Island, where Robert Louis Stevenson played as a child. Local lore is that the island inspired him to write the book "Treasure Island." The island can be reached by walking to it at low tide.

There are several small cafes and inns located in Cramond. The Cramond Inn was a favorite of Stevenson's.

The Cramond Cafe is a small quaint one room cafe featuring wonderful homemade desserts and soups. The 16th-century stone dining room has a large picture window that offers a stunning view of the harbor as you sip sweet warm chocolate.

There are several small shops where you can purchase souvenirs of your visit. As you make your way back to the bus stop you will want to visit the remains of a Roman fort that dates back to the second century. These remnants are from the very edge of the Roman Empire at its height of power in Britain.

There are many motels and bed and breakfast hotels to stay in during your visit to Edinburgh. Most bed and breakfast hotels offer a hearty home-cooked breakfast as well as a friendly atmosphere.

You can obtain a list of bed and breakfast hotels by writing or calling the Edinburgh and Scotland Information Centre, 3 Princess Street, Edinburgh, Scotland. Phone 031-557-1700.

The center will also be able to supply you with maps and brochures about Edinburgh and its wonderful sights.

Edinburgh is full of things to see and do and you could easily spend your whole time in Scotland there, but if you want to venture to other destinations, trains are available on a regular schedule and there are two train stations to serve you. The Waverly station is the main station and Haymarket is the second station that offers limited service.

A few tips while in Edinburgh:

- Invest in a lightweight all weather jacket. Scotland's weather can be unpredictable and light showers are a daily occurrence.
- Have plenty of change on hand when riding the bus. Bus drivers do not make change.
- Pack comfortable shoes and clothing. The weather can become quite chilly even in the middle of summer.
- Carry a card with your hotel address on it in case you get lost.
- Purchase a good map of the city listing its sights and points of interest. Some of the hotels supply their guests with complimentary maps and brochures.

Source: *Travel* Magazine, Jan. 1996, with permission.

APPENDIX
D

First Draft:

"Waterskiing at Its Ultimate," by Jennifer Wittwer

Think of waterskiing at speeds exceeding 75 mph. and then imagine skiing at those speeds for an hour straight. This isn't just a demented rumination (crazy thought) for National Champion Speed-Skier, Corey Cook—it's his life.

Cook has been racing at minimum speeds of 65 mph. since he was only eleven years old and he has been a top skier ever since.

Speedskiing is not a widely known sport here in the U.S. but it is growing and with the interest the media is taking in this sport it is sure to gain the attention and popularity it richly deserves. For those who are involved in the sport at all levels and those who have attended a ski-race event know the the thrill and excitement of the competitions. Many have become addicted to the sport, one of the many is Cook.

Cook is a Southern California native and still enjoys living there. It has been a perfect location, being close to the ocean and various small lakes allowing plenty of practice territory. Yet, Cook is seldom home during ski race season, March through November, because he is off to the races. Whether the races are as far South as San Diego or as far North as Clear Lake, Corey and his racing team are there.

Cook is fortunate to have his father as a part of his team. His father, Terry Cook, observes for Corey. Each ski race team consists of a boat driver, an observer, sometimes a navigator (depending upon the race) and of course a skier. Each member of the team is very important and they all contribute to how well the skier can do. Not only is Terry Corey's observer and a large part of his success, but he is the person who got Cook involved in ski racing as well as helps keep him motivated to train and succeed.

During the U.S. ski racing "off-season", Corey visits other countries where it is ski race season, such as Australia. Cook has raced some of the biggest races in Australia for the past 8 years and even holds the winning titles to a number of them. He is a two time Australian International Champion and the New South Wales, Australian Men's State Champion. Corey says he enjoys racing in Australia because there is extremely tough competition and many challenging race courses, in addition this helps to keep him in shape for the U.S. season.

Among many other awards, some of Cook's most outstanding accomplishments include: 4 time USA Mens National Champion, 6 time USA High-Point Champion and 2 time Alcatraz-San Francisco Bay Challenge Winner (and includes being the current record holder for this race). Cook also set the Jr. Boys time record for the Catalina Ski Race in 1987, when he was 14 years old and the record has not been touched since.

Every 2 years, there are the "World Titles" (waterskiing's answer to the Olympics), in which the top skiers from all over the world come together to compete for the World Championship Title. To be a part of the World Team is a prestigious honor and privilege, since only 4 men and 4 women from each country are chosen to represent their respective countries. Corey is a 3 time USA World Team member. That means he was only 16 years old when he went to represent our Country at his first world titles, which were held in Como, Italy. Corey has also been to Darwin, Australia as well as France to compete in the World Title Competitions. August 1995, the USA team will once again compete in the World Titles being held in Belgium, for which Corey hopes to be a selected team member.

Although Corey has many accomplishments, he still has quite a few goals to reach. His biggest goal is to bring home the gold from Belgium, making him "World Champion". He has also been a top competitor in the famous Catalina Ski Race, where around 100+ competitors race in the Ocean off Long Beach, Calif. to Catalina Island and back (52 miles approximately). He strives to bring home the 1st place overall trophy in the Catalina Race and is encouraged to do so soon. Australia's biggest race, the "Bridge to Bridge", which is a 72 mile race with over 200 entrants on average, is another race Corey has been a top finisher in for a number of years and has his sights set to win. Corey's goal is not just to be one of the best, but to be the very best.

Cook has a strong competitive heart and loves tough competition. He admits that he hates to lose, but accepts a loss when he feels he gave it his best. Usually if Corey gives it his best and the boat he's behind keeps up, he doesn't have to worry about losing.

Corey maintains a rigorous daily work out, which includes weight training, excer-cycle, as well as Mountain Biking and water-skiing at least 2–3 hours per week. Corey has a small T-shirt silk screen business which affords him the flexibility to train and compete.

Corey has many people he admires in the sport from drivers to observers to fellow skiers. When asked who he would consider to be his mentor in the sport Corey said it was not one but two people in the sport of speed ski-racing; Kurt Schoen, four time overall winner of the prestigious Catalina Ski Race, and Mike Avila, both U.S. World Class skiers.

Source: Jennifer Wittwer, with permission.

Editor's Notes

Jonathan Cullimore, managing editor of *The Water Skier*, wanted more information about Corey Cook. With a few phone calls he obtained the following quotes:

- Terry Cook:

  "He's a real hard trainer."

  "When he was younger, he progressed quickly. Now that he's at the top, he just has to keep his physical condition up."

  "John Bowles is a strong competitor."

  "The Catalina race brings people out of the woodwork that pose strong competition."

- John Bohls:

  "He blows my doors off!"

  "I've been racing Corey for a number of years, and he's incredible. He's incredibly fast."

  "My goal is to ski the absolute best and fastest ever."

  "Corey is an incredible skier. He's always been tremendously fast."

  "He's a true athlete and a good sportsman. He's got the true athletic spirit."

- Randy Davis:

  "In the last two years there hasn't been anybody who could beat him. He's become really relaxed and started having more fun while he's out there skiing."

  "With anything, it's as much mental as it is physical. He's just become so much more relaxed."

  "He can compete with anybody in the world."

APPENDIX

Final Draft:

"Waterskiing at Its Ultimate," by Jennifer Wittwer

Think of water skiing at speeds exceeding 75 mph, then imagine skiing at those speeds for an hour straight. This isn't just a determined rumination for national champion speed skier Corey Cook—it's his life!

Cook has been racing at minimum speeds of 65 mph since he was 11 years old, and has been a top competitor ever since.

"Corey is an incredible skier. He's always been tremendously fast," says John Bohls, a fellow ski racer and one of Cook's closest competitors. "He blows my doors off!"

Speed skiing is not only a widely known sport here in the United States, but those involved know the thrill and excitement of the competition. Many, like Cook, have become addicted to the sport.

Cook is a southern California native who says he enjoys living close to the ocean and various small lakes that offer him plenty of practice territory. March through November, though, he is rarely home. A hectic ski race season schedule keeps him on the road, and whether the races are as far south as San Diego or as far north as Clear Lake, Cook and his racing team are there.

Each ski race team consists of a boat driver, an observer, sometimes a navigator (depending on the race) and the skier. Each team member contributes to the skier's performance, and one major team advantage Cook has is his father, Terry Cook, as an observer. More than anyone, Terry Cook was responsible for getting Corey involved in ski racing. He helps motivate him to train and succeed.

"He's a real hard trainer," says Terry. "When he was younger he progressed very quickly. Now that he's at the top, he just has to keep his physical condition up."

Randy Davis, one of Cook's drivers, says that Cook has the attitude of a winner.

"In the last two years, there just hasn't been anybody who could beat him," says Davis. "He's become really relaxed and started having more fun while he's out there skiing."

During his off-season in the U.S., Cook visits other countries, such as Australia, to observe their ski racers and compete. For eight years, he has raced in some of the largest tournaments in Australia, winning a number of them. He is two-time Australian International Champion and the New South Wales, Australia, Men's State Champion. He says he enjoys racing Australia's tough competitors and challenging courses, because it keeps him in shape for the U.S. season.

Some of Cook's most outstanding accomplishments include: four-time U.S. Men's National Champion; six-time U.S. High-Point Champion; and two-time Alcatraz–San Francisco Bay Challenge winner (he is current record holder for this race). At age 14, Cook set the Junior Boys time record for the Catalina Ski Race in 1987, and his record still stands.

Every two years there are the world events, in which top skiers from all over the world come together to compete for the world championship title. To be a part of a world team is a prestigious honor, since only four men and four women from each country are chosen to represent their respective nations. Cook, a three-time U.S. World Team member, was only 16 years old when he went to represent the United States at his first world title event in Como, Italy. He has competed in Darwin, Australia, and France and has been a top competitor in the famous Catalina Ski Race, where approximately 150 skiers race in the ocean off Long Beach, Calif., to Catalina Island and back—a 52-mile round trip. In August, the U.S. Team will compete in the World Ski Race Championships in Belgium.

Although Cook has accomplished a great deal, he still claims to have quite a few goals to reach. His main goal, he says, is to bring home a gold medal from Belgium. He continuously strives for the first-place overall trophy in the Catalina Race, and he has set his sights to win Australia's biggest race, the Bridge to Bridge. This 72-mile race features on average 200 competitors, and Cook has been a top finisher for a number of years.

Cook keeps himself in shape with a rigorous daily workout which includes weight training, using an exercise bike, mountain biking and water skiing at least two to three hours a week. Cook owns a small T-shirt silk-screen business which affords him the flexibility to train and compete.

From drivers to observers to fellow skiers, Cook has many people in water skiing he admires. When asked who he would consider to be his mentor in the sport, Cook mentions two world-class ski racers—Kurt Schoen, four-time overall winner of the Catalina Ski Race, and Mike Avila.

"I've looked up to Kurt and Mike for the last 15 years," says Cook. "They were the top performers when I started racing. They were the record setters and that's where I had set my goals."

Cook also says that he admired the late Kirk Book for his competitive spirit and dedication to the sport of ski racing.

Source: The article, "Water Skiing at Its Ultimate" is reprinted with permission of the American Water Ski Association from *The Water Skier* magazine, page 26, copyright June/July 1995.

USAA Brochure

Welcome to USAA's Southeast Regional Office

Since 1973, we've been serving the insurance claims and policy service needs of USAA members in the southeastern states and the Caribbean. As our membership base has grown and capabilities expanded, we've become one of Tampa's largest employers.

At USAA, success comes from focusing on our members, but our focus isn't singular. We care about our employees, too. We know that only those people who feel a sense of pride and responsibility can deliver premier service. So we've designed a work environment that creates the conditions for excellence: pleasant, healthy, and worker-friendly. Employees enjoy everything from ergonomically correct chairs to working out in the fitness center.

Our commitment extends to the Tampa Bay community. We have an active Volunteer Corps which donates thousands of hours of time each year to worthy causes—everything from painting the homes of the economically disadvantaged to joining area walk-a-thons to support various worthwhile causes.

We're proud to be members of this community and to be known as good corporate citizens. We have grown with this community, and this office building is a solid and proud commitment to Tampa's future.

> Joseph House
> Colonel (Ret.) USA
> *Regional Vice President*

USAA built its reputation on a tradition of responsiveness, dependability and quality service. Helping to keep that time-honored mission alive are the men and women of USAA's Southeast Regional Office (SERO).

The Tampa facility is one of six regional offices located across the U.S. and Europe. Established in 1973 with a staff of 36 people, SERO initially served USAA members in Florida and Alabama. Over the years, its responsibilities expanded to serve the insurance claims and policy service needs of members in eight southeastern states and Puerto Rico, the Virgin Islands, the Bahamas and Guantanamo Bay, Cuba. By the end of 1994, the office had grown to more than 1,500 employees.

In a best-selling book published in 1993, USAA was named one of the top 10 companies to work for in America. The book called USAA "a safe harbor where employees have incredible opportunities." Those opportunities include having access to the latest technology to better serve members; a well-planned, attractive, and productive work environment, and an emphasis on continuous training to further build and develop a top-notch workforce.

A History of Service

Through its more than 75 subsidiaries and affiliate companies, USAA offers a full spectrum of insurance and financial services, including property and casualty insurance, life and health insurance, no-load mutual funds, real estate investment, a discount brokerage and banking services. It is the nation's fifth-largest insurer of private automobiles and the fourth-largest homeowners insurer. Also available to members are a buying service and travel agency.

Founded in 1922 by a group of Army officers, USAA has become one of the country's most respected corporations and is ranked among *Fortune* magazine's top 50 diversified financial services companies. The company was formed because military officers, with their transitory lifestyles, often had a difficult time finding automobile insurance.

Today, more than 95 percent of active duty military officers are USAA members, and the tradition of service continues.

As part of a member-owned reciprocal insurance exchange, members insured one another, sharing the risks and the rewards. As the company grew and prospered, additional lines of insurance and financial services were added.

Worldwide, USAA serves more than 2.6 million members. Members are generally commissioned or warrant officers in the U.S. Armed Forces, or special agents with the FBI, U.S. Treasury Department or Naval Investigative Services who are on active duty, in the Reserves or National Guard, retired or separated from service. Associate members, eligible for automobile and property insurance, are former dependent children, grandchildren, spouses and ex-spouses of USAA members.

About Our Facility

The Tampa office of USAA rests on a 128-acre site in an area of town known as New Tampa, just off Bruce B. Downs Boulevard at I-75. The seven-story, 529,000-square-foot building became home to SERO employees late in 1993. It features a cafeteria, health clinic, fitness center and an outside recreation area across the 20-acre lake which graces the front of the building.

Abundant natural light filters into the work areas to provide a pleasant and productive environment. At breaktime, many people don tennis shoes for a brisk walk along the path that wraps around the lake, enjoying all the wildlife which has taken up residence there.

USAA is committed to building and maintaining a quality workforce, so training and continuing education classes are always available. There are 22 classrooms at SERO with skilled in-house trainers offering instruction in a wide array of topics, including insurance, delivering quality service and computer technology.

Most USAA members conduct their business with the company over the phone, but there are occasions when a personal visit is in order. To make face-to-face meetings convenient, walk-in offices are located on the first floor of the building, just behind the main lobby. There, members can talk with claims and policy service representatives, as well as USAA financial services professionals. Members may also come on site for the Drive-in Claims facility, which performs automobile damage appraisals.

Source: Reprinted with permission of USAA Property and Casualty Insurance.

G

"Girls with ADD,"
by Jeannette Batz

By the time she was 10 years old, Corinne Olson was *impossible*. Every Monday before school, she faked being sick to try to get out of going. Whenever her parents asked her to do something—clean up her room, set the table for dinner—she would snap, *"I'm not going to do it, and there's no way you can make me!"* The fights that followed were often fierce.

Corinne's behavior got so extreme that her parents took her to a psychologist. The conclusion: She was trying to "control the family" and would change only if there were "logical consequences" to her acting out. So one evening when she refused to set the table, the rest of the family went out to a restaurant, leaving her at home. Corinne flew into a rage and trashed the kitchen.

Logical consequences or not, Corinne wasn't changing, so her parents sought another opinion. When she was finishing fifth grade, Corinne was diagnosed with Attention Deficit Disorder, or ADD. Her parents learned that when their perfectly capable and intelligent daughter said she *wouldn't* do something, it meant she *couldn't*—ADD made it impossible for her to focus on the task.

Corinne told her mom later: "You know, if you had taken a paper place mat, drawn in the positions of the plate, knife, fork, and napkin, and posted it on the fridge, I could have done it. But when you just said, 'Set the table,' well, I could never remember to put the place mat down first."

Corinne's family started to deal with her more patiently, and she started taking Ritalin—a stimulant that can act like 12 cups of coffee for someone without the disorder but helps people with ADD focus and concentrate.

Corinne is now 18 and a freshman at Hobart & William Smith College, in Geneva, New York. She's a member of her school's cross-country team, and she plans to study learning disabilities and childhood development.

"It's not like you wake up one morning and say, 'Oh, I have ADD, but I'm okay,'" Corinne says. "What happens is you grow up. Now I'm kind of glad I have it. This is basically a J.Crew campus. Everyone is beautiful and everyone looks the same. If you have ADD, you learn to pride yourself on being different, instead of getting upset about it."

Basically, ADD distorts the way the brain sends and receives messages. The pattern of symptoms changes with each individual. Some kids are distracted, quiet, and dreamy; others talk incessantly and are given to impulsive bursts of energy, anger, or both.

"You know those new Magnavox TVs that show 15 channels at once so that you can decide which one you want to watch without channel surfing?" Corinne asks. "Because I have ADD, the option for me to choose one screen is, like, impossible. I keep moving from picture to picture—and as a result I don't know what's going on in any of them."

Until now, guys have been diagnosed with ADD at a much higher rate than girls. This is mainly because hyperactivity is the most common—and obvious—tip-off that someone might have ADD, and guys tend to be a lot more hyper than girls. But now doctors think that ADD may be much more common among girls than previously believed.

Dr. Edward Hallowell, a psychiatrist who has ADD himself and is a coauthor of two books about it, writes that probably 15 million children and adults in this country have ADD, but "a lot of girls who have it never get diagnosed. Instead, they're just thought of as shy or quiet or even depressed."

Girls with ADD often turn the disorder's strong, impulsive feelings in on themselves. They drift off to dreamland, bounce from one distraction to the next, or get depressed—symptoms all the girls interviewed for this story said they were familiar with. And each of the seven psychiatrists and psychologists we consulted agreed that girls with ADD often receive inadequate treatment or no treatment at all.

According to Kate Kelly and Peggy Ramundo, who cowrote the book *You Mean I'm Not Lazy, Stupid or Crazy?* (Scribner, 1995) after learning they had ADD: "Historically, six times more boys than girls have been diagnosed with the disorder. The ratio is more like one-to-one if ADD without hyperactivity is included."

Too Much Attention or Not Enough?

Everybody has trouble paying attention in class, but if you have ADD, it's a hundred times harder to concentrate. Instead of screening out the background, your brain is paying attention to everything at once, zigzagging after every noise or movement. Even though it's called Attention *Deficit* Disorder, the problem may really be that you pay too *much* attention. You can't stop receiving messages from the outside world.

"You try *so hard* to pay attention, but you just *can't*," says Christy Rade, a 14-year-old from West Des Moines, Iowa, who learned she had ADD when she was in third grade. "You keep on thinking about other things and you can't hear the teacher talking—it's like you go deaf or something. You try to focus, but you keep spacing off. You might click back for a minute or two, but it's like there are different channels, and you know the boring one's going to help you someday, but you keep switching it. You're going, 'Oh, man, I just missed that, didn't I?' You come back and the teacher's done talking and you have to ask other people what she said."

The weird part is that people with ADD are often able to "hyperfocus." They lock in on a task and can't stop, even if they're spending way too much time on details that won't matter in the long run or their teacher's trying to get them to move on to the next subject.

This can work against people with ADD, but it also can be an advantage. Many are passionate about one interest and intensely creative. "Every single person I know with ADD is really good at one thing," Corinne notes. She recalls learning soon after her diagnoses that a lot of highly motivated, successful people have ADD. "A lot of athletes, musicians, actors, and actresses have it," Corinne says. "When you hear that, and you see what great things these people have done, it's an incredible relief. You know that you can succeed at whatever you choose to do."

Space Cadets, Rude Girls, Motormouths

ADD doesn't show up the same way in all girls. It makes Christy spacey and distracted; people used to call her a "dizzy blond," a "space cadet." She remembers one day in particular: "In third grade, my favorite teacher told me I was blaming my problems on everybody else when they were really all my fault. I burst into tears. . . . It's *always* been hard for me to pay attention."

Corinne gets really hyper and can't stop talking. Her childhood nickname was "motormouth," and she has always been spontaneous, blurting out her feelings without filtering them. "I was *never* shy," she says, "and sometimes that intimidated people and drove them away."

The good news is that Ritalin helps both Christy and Corinne deal. "It relaxes me so I can pay attention," Christy says. "Before, I just thought I was dumb. Now I don't drift off anymore." Corinne says she feels a definite difference without the medicine: "I'm all over the place. I can't sit down, I'm the center of the crowd, getting all the attention. On Ritalin, I still have a lot of energy—I can still jump around and be funny—but I'm more focused."

Corinne is energetic—after a day of attending classes, she can run cross-country, go to a party, and be ready for more. But she says she's also moody and easily depressed. That's common with ADD. The reason is probably partly chemical and partly frustration: Girls with ADD work harder to stay tuned in. Depression hits some girls so hard they withdraw, blaming themselves for problems that are really caused by ADD. They play a constant tape inside their head that says what a screwup, goofball, klutz, or loser they are. They feel out of control in the world because they're out of control inside. So they take a stubborn stand, opposing whatever a parent wants, contradicting whatever a friend says.

After living with ADD for eight years, 16-year-old Jennifer Creasy, a preacher's daughter from Bedford, Virginia, can tell when it's making her "kind of obnoxious. I'm really hyper, out of control. If my mom asks me to do something, I'll complain a lot and won't do it right away, and she'll have to ask me a few times, because I don't listen."

This stubbornness, too, can be softened by Ritalin. Stacy Conant, a 13-year-old with ADD from Bellevue, Washington, says, "It makes me happy, more willing to do things. If I wasn't taking it, someone would ask me, 'Would you do this for me?'—just a simple little thing—and I'd go, 'No!' When I'm taking it, I say, 'Sure!' "

Even on Ritalin, things aren't always smooth. An only child, Jennifer admits she generally has a hard time dealing with her mother. She blames ADD, in part, but says, "I think it's normal mother-daughter stuff."

"I have my down days," Jennifer continues, "when I think everybody's against me. But I think that's pretty normal, too. It's not like I sit in my room all day, bumming about having ADD. I'm more likely to be listening to Reba McEntire. I'm generally a pretty happy person."

Sometimes girls with ADD dread any kind of failure; they feel like they've failed too much already—trying hard to slide through a world that wasn't built for ADD—and they respond by blaming everybody *but* themselves. They can be irritable because their thin concentration is constantly getting interrupted; they can be abrupt to the point of rudeness, because their mind is already racing to the next message. And they can be smartass-sarcastic sometimes, too, because it's such a great cover-up for shame.

"I got in trouble a lot," says Stacy. "One time I almost got suspended for talking back to the teachers. I was really angry." What made her angry were usually simple little everyday annoyances that, if she were able to relax, would go away in a few minutes. But she felt like she had to let the anger out. "I know I hurt some people by getting angry," she says. "But I get so frustrated and mad sometimes, I just have to do something aggressive."

In his first book on the subject, *Driven to Distraction* (Pantheon, 1994), Dr. Hallowell writes: "People with ADD may not make friends or do well socially simply because *they don't know how.* They don't know the rules. They don't know the steps of the dance." The rest of us don't have to be taught those steps; they come naturally, and we assume everybody knows them. But once someone with ADD figures out where her feet go, the awkwardness dissolves and her personality emerges.

First diagnosed with ADD at age four, Stacy says she was depressed for much of her childhood. She dealt with her depression by overeating. But just last year, she started taking Ritalin. Now she says her attitude is changing, and the weight is dropping off. "I felt very, very sad before, like no one wanted to be my friend, no one loved me," she says. "The thing that loved me back was food, so that's how I got to be overweight. Now, if I call someone and they can't do something, I don't immediately assume they don't want to be with me, I just think maybe they already had plans."

Roller-coaster IQ

When you hear that someone is "learning disabled" (LD), you might immediately conclude that she's "dumb" or "slow." Not so: People with learning disabilities (including ADD) are often very intelligent—they just have a problem (it could be physical *or* mental) that limits their school performance. "When people make fun of someone who is LD," Jennifer says, "it makes me mad. I say, 'Hey, *I'm* LD!' I get A's and B's in school. It just takes me a little bit longer." Completing a test or assignment itself doesn't necessarily take longer, she explains, "It just takes extra time to focus and get started."

Christy says, "It's always taken me a while to *get* things, but once I get them, I really remember them." The year after she found out about ADD, she worked with a math tutor and discovered she could do long division just fine, provided she could follow someone through the material at her own pace. In high school, Corinne used two tutors: During her sophomore year, she had a history tutor who also helped her with study and organizational skills; junior year she had a Latin tutor.

When people with ADD take intelligence tests, their scores graph like a roller coaster: They peak in one area, dip low on the chart, then rise again. ADD is one good reason you can't say somebody is smart or stupid, a genius or a moron—we all have several different levels of intelligence and show our skills in different ways.

ADD can cause problems with math and spelling, but that's more common with boys than girls—which is another reason girls don't get diagnosed as easily. A specific, traditional learning disability might occur alongside ADD— someone might have trouble unscrambling a string of words, finding the right word, remembering language, or writing it down. But ADD itself occurs in the brightest people—Dr. Hallowell thinks Mozart, Ben Franklin, and Thomas Edison probably had ADD, and Dustin Hoffman has it.

Which One's the Real Me?

The right medicine can ease most of ADD's symptoms. But there's been so much concern and misinformation about Ritalin and other ADD medicines (for instance, the antidepressant Zoloft) that many parents don't explore them.

Ritalin, for one, can take your appetite, disturb your sleep, or make you restless and agitated. (Psychiatrists say that for most of their patients those side effects ease in about a month, as the body adjusts.)

Even when the medicine improves your life, it's hard to *have* to take it. Ritalin wears off in a few hours, so you usually need it several times a day—which makes other people curious. "A kid in my class was on Ritalin," Corinne remembers, "and people called it the hyper pill. I *really* didn't want the teacher to say out loud to me, 'Go take your Ritalin.'"

Jennifer still remembers the day in fourth grade when she "had to take the Ritalin during lunch, and this kid called me a drug addict." Now she has come to terms with the medicine: "If I take it, I do well in school, and if I don't take it, I do poorly."

Corinne says that whenever she has a burst of energy, "people ask me if I've forgotten my 'Rit,' as my dad calls it. I can't express myself or be overly energetic without somebody reminding me to take Ritalin.

"It's weird," Corinne continues. "This little pill totally changes who I am—but not really. I'm chemically unbalanced, and Ritalin gives me the chemicals I need." As Dr. Hallowell points out, medicine doesn't live your life or do your work for you; it just "evens the playing field."

How Other People Can Help

Having ADD means needing to be constantly aware of how it affects you, so it helps to have a few good friends to keep you in check. "If I'm in class with a friend who knows about my ADD, and I start spacing out, she'll just kick my desk or something to wake me up," Christy says with a laugh.

Getting your friends to understand is fairly easy, but teachers can be a little harder to educate. Jennifer says one of her fifth grade teachers decided that she "was just a discipline case. My mom went to her and explained. Once the teacher found out, she treated me a lot differently because she knew I couldn't help it." Stacy remembers a teacher who raked her over the coals—then learned more about ADD, changed the way she treated Stacy, and even spread the word to other faculty.

"A lot of teachers will make students feel stupid or embarrass them in front of the class," complains Corinne. "That interferes with a lot of girls' self-esteem. It's harder for girls to fit in than guys; girls have all these little cliques, plus they worry what the guys think of them." It's inexcusable for teachers to say anything about ADD in front of the rest of the class, Corinne adds, but if they do, "you should tell them how you feel about privacy. A lot of kids don't think they have that option."

Parents matter most—their attitude can make or break a daughter's struggle with ADD. " 'Try harder' is the worst thing you can say to a child with ADD," says Corinne's mom, Judy Olson. "It just increases the anxiety."

Dr. Dean Rosen, a St. Louis psychologist and ADD specialist, advises parents to focus on developing their daughter's strengths, instead of trying to correct her "flaws" or the "deficit" in her attention. Parents should not take their daughter's angry outbursts personally, or analyze them while they're happening. Above all, parents should give immediate feedback—and remember that praise often falls on deaf ears, so they'll have to repeat it.

Seven years after she was diagnosed with ADD, Corinne says she has come to terms with it—well, almost. Having to rely on Ritalin constantly is a pain, and sometimes she gets really annoyed when people don't understand her. "I've learned to live with it, but that doesn't mean it doesn't make me angry sometimes," she says.

One person who *does* understand is her boyfriend of two years, a student at Dartmouth College in Hanover, New Hampshire. "He's totally helped me with this," she says. "He knows, for instance, that I can get lost in talking—it's one of my favorite things to do, and my ADD makes me even *more* talkative—but he'll say, 'Corinne, you really need to start doing your homework now. Let's get off the phone.'

"It's a little thing, I know," she says. "But the little things add up."

Do You Have ADD?

Just because you can't pay attention or feel restless some-times doesn't mean you have ADD. But you *might* if you consistently:

- have trouble paying attention to details.
- are unable to focus on something for a long time.
- fail to listen closely or follow instructions.
- leave schoolwork, projects, or chores unfinished.
- are unable to organize yourself, your activities, your possessions.
- fidget with your hands, hair, or feet.
- feel restless and can't sit still.
- have trouble entertaining yourself quietly.
- talk too much.
- stay "on the go" and feel "driven."
- interrupt people when they're speaking.
- have trouble waiting your turn.

To find out more, call Children and Adults with Attention Deficit Disorders (CHADD) at 800-233-4050.

Source: *Seventeen* Magazine, Jan. 1995, with permission.

First Draft:

"The Scene on Bayshore," by D. Quentin Wilber

Joan Routt races down Bayshore Boulevard's sidewalk, barely visible beneath her black floppy brimmed hat, black plastic knee guards and black velcro wrist braces.

Her black in-line skates clackety-clack across the pavement before she bumps into the balustrade. Sweat drips from her shadowed chin in the early Saturday heat. It's 8 a.m., and like most of the skaters, joggers, runners and bikers on Bayshore's sidewalk she wants to work-out before the sun rises any higher.

And while out here to skate, Routt, like a growing number of Bayshore enthusiats, wouldn't mind meeting that someone special in the process.

"I'm too old for that pick up stuff," she says, swiping her cheek with a wrist guard. ""If I saw Mr. Right, I probably couldn't catch him. If he caught me, that would be O.K."

With recent publicity from Felicia Haber's book, "Florida Men," which lists Bayshore a top spot to pick up a heath concious guy, from newspaper articles and the word of mouth, this 9.3 mile stretch along the Bay is gaining the reputation of a pick up artist's paradise.

One man calls it the longest singles bar in the Tampa area. Another says several enquiring women have asked for his telephone number. And one woman calls it happy hour and refuses to walk without her husband on weekdays.

But even with that racy stigma, most exercisers say you get a better idea of whom you're meeting here than in the night clubs and bars.

"They're sober, you're sober, and you're seeing them at their worst, sweaty, smelly, natural," says Margaret O'Grady, who already ran at 6 a.m. and is now skating for fun two hours later. She says this is a perfect place to meet someone who shares her desire to keep fit.

"This is good, you might be able to judge their character better," O'Grady says, her shirt already soaked with sweat. "You might not be able to catch the real character of someone in a bar or some other place."

At 9: a.m., the crowd thickening along the balustrade, the skaters weave in and out among the stream of people. Calls of "coming on your left," blast unexpectedly from zooming bikers.

In the water, a dorsal fin breaks the ripples, then another. A father peers at the Bay, his two children resting in a three-wheels, pink stroller. He points at something and says, "Look, there are some manatee." His young daughter shrieks.

Sandy Huston, walking her two golden dogs toward the sound end of Bayshore, says she wouldn't mind finding a man. "I get a lot of attention from the dogs," she says. "The people out here enjoy the same things. The water, the exercise, I'm looking everywhere all the time."

"This would be husband number 3, so you have to be careful."

A lot of looking, a lot of peeking, but not too much talking, it seems. But don't tell that to Windy Evans. She says she won't even come out here after work on weekdays.

"I all it happy hour, that's why I only come out here on Saturday and Sunday mornings," she says, hurring hom after a long walk. "After work, around 6:30, it's packed mostly. If I do come out here, I bring my husband. People whistle and make comments."

Around 6:30 is when the action starts, the exercisers say. That's when most of the pick up artists do their thing.

It's 6 p.m. Monday as the evening crowd settles into its different paces. The pavement burns, but a slight Bay breeze cools the sweating bodies.

Shirt-less roller-bladers Brue Brovillete, 33, and Scott Wisker, 32, have their own theories about this so-called pick up mecca.

'It seems like a good place, a lot of eye contact," Brovillete says. "It's Florida, people like flesh."

Wisker, deftly blading back and forth, says this is the perfect location to meet "the skantily clad, exercising and sweaty" type.

Adjusting the brakes on his bike, Brian Yelvington says he's had girls approach him before. "They ask me that my name is," he says. "I gave them my phone number. But none of them have called."

But unlike Yelvington, others have been using Bayshore for years and never even noticed a single phone number exchange.

Running down the sidewalk, darting in and out of the walkers, Cindy Thurber refuses to stop. No, she hasn't noticed the social scene, she says.

"I've been jogging it for three years," Thurber says between breaths. "Nobody's picked me up."

And then, almost out of ear shot, they thity-three year old yells, ""I wish they did."

It's too hot for the dolphins and the manatees today. Streams of people walk across from Hyde Park while others emerge in the distance along the boulevard's sidewalk. The car traffic picks up. The rubbery, hollow thumpety, thump of tires striking cement reaches the sidewalk.

Many exercise eeyday at the same time, leading one man to compare the crowd to a big family. And while most of the publicity has focused on finding a date, Russ Callahan says he met his good friend nancy here two years ago.

"I happened to notice her exercising," says Callahan, walking shirtless in the early evening heat. "One thing led to another, a friendship began. This is a focal point for this kind of activity onthe south part of town. It's exercise combined with a nice social envoronment you wouldn't find other places."

Many probably don't notice the social possibilities, says Callahan, because they're so into their exercise. " "It wouldn't surprise me that people don't notice it," he says, picking up his pace. " "When you're exercising, you're relaxed, unconscious of what's going on around you."

Groups of two and three predominate tonight. Engaged in animate conversation, arms gesticulating, they don't seem interested in meeting new people.

"We see the same group of people out here," says Jennifer Reina, her companion Dana Caranante nodding in agreement. "for us we do it mostly to work out."

"Sometimes we say hello and greet people," adds Caranante before she and Reina quicken their pace.

Source: D. Quentin Wilber, with permission.

APPENDIX

I

Final Draft:

"The Scene on Bayshore," by D. Quentin Wilber

Barely visible beneath her black, floppy brimmed hat, black plastic knee guard and black Velcro wrist braces, Joan Routt races down Bayshore Boulevard's sidewalk.

Her black in-line skates clackety-clack over the pavement as she arcs toward the balustrade Bam!

With her blades tilted toward, this bookkeeper from Lutz braces against the railing and spins slowly from Hillsborough Bay. Sweat streaks down shadowed cheeks and chin in the 8 a.m. Saturday heat.

Zeeeepppphhhh, a male bicyclist zips by, and then, several seconds later, glances inquisitively at Routt. Not surprising.

For some time, Bayshore's regulars have been calling this "the longest singles bar in Tampa." Author Felicia Michele Haber of Hollywood, Fla., even mentions it in her new book, "Florida Men: A Road Atlas for Single Women," as the best place to meet men who jog or go in-line skating.

But many here simply think of it as a health-conscious flirter's paradise.

"I'm too old for that pickup stuff," the 55-year-old Routt says, brushing her cheek with a wrist guard. "If I saw Mr.

Right, I probably couldn't catch him. If he caught me, that would be OK."

Under the clear sun and fluffy clouds, with Tampa's skyline in the distance, all types of people seek out Bayshore Boulevard.

"Bayshore is a very unique and charming location," says Anne Freeman of the Greater Tampa Chamber of Commerce. "It's the world's longest continuous sidewalk where people enjoy wandering and taking evening strolls."

But this morning, mostly sweating singles pound down the 6-mile stretch of pavement. Here, they have found a perfect alternative to the nightclub and bar scene.

"They're sober, you're sober, and you're seeing them at their worst — sweaty, smelly, natural," says Margaret O'Grady, who already ran at 6 a.m. and is skating for fun two hours later.

The 28-year-old accountant says Bayshore is the place to meet someone who shares her desire to keep fit.

"This is good: You might be able to judge their character better," she says, her shirt soaked with perspiration. "You might not be able to catch the real character of someone in a bar or some other place."

At 9 a.m., as the crowd thickens along the balustrade, skaters and bikers zoom among the streams of people. Shouts of "Coming on your left" startle the unsuspecting. In the water a dorsal fin breaks the ripples. Then another. A father peers at the dolphins, his two children resting in a three-wheeled, pink stroller.

Toward the south end of the boulevard, Sandy Huston, 55, walks her two dogs, a golden retriever and a mixed breed. She says this would be a great place to meet a man, next to the water, under the blue sky.

"I get a lot of attention because of the dogs," says Huston, an interior designer. "The people out here enjoy the same things — the water, the exercise. I'm looking everywhere all the time.

"This would be husband No. 3, so you have to be careful."

■ ■ ■

On weekday evenings, the scene gets even hotter.

It's 8 p.m. this Monday as the evening crowd settles into its different paces. The pavement burns, but a breeze cools the sweating bodies.

Shirtless skaters Bruce Brovillete, 33, and Scott Wisker, 32, have their own theories about this place.

"It seems like a good place, a lot of eye contact," Brovillete says. "It's Florida; people like flesh."

Wisker, deftly blading back and forth, says this is the perfect location to meet "the scantily clad, exercising and sweaty" type.

Adjusting the brakes on his bike, warehouse manager Brian Yelvington says women have cornered him before.

"They ask me what my name is," he says. "I gave them my phone number. But none of them have called."

It almost feels too hot for the dolphins today. Streams of people cross the road from Hyde Park while others emerge to the distance along the boulevard's sidewalk. Traffic rushes by, as the rubbery, hollow thumpety-thump of tires striking concrete reaches the sidewalk.

Many have exercised at the same hour for months, even years, the exercisers say.

"You see a lot of the same people out here," says dentist Joe Martineau, 57. "The skaters are together, the bikers ride together. It's one big family."

Russ Callahan agrees. He says he met his good friend Nancy here two years ago.

"I happened to notice her exercising," says Callahan, 44, walking shirtless in the early evening heat. "One thing led to another (and) a friendship began."

Many probably miss the social possibilities because they're so into working out, says Callahan, a vice president at Legg Mason Real Estate Services.

"It wouldn't surprise me that people don't notice it," he says, picking up the pace. "When you're exercising, you're relaxed, unconscious of what's going on around you."

Groups of two and three predominate tonight. Engaged in animated conversation, arms gesticulating, they seem totally engrossed with each other.

"We see the same group of people out here," says Jennifer Reina, 29, her friend Dana Caranante nodding in agreement. "For us, we do it mostly to work out."

"Sometimes we say hello and greet people," adds Caranante, 29, before she and Reina quicken their pace and walk away.

Running down the sidewalk, darting in and out of walkers, Cindy Thurber refuses to stop. No, the 33-year-old hasn't noticed the social scene, she says.

"I've been jogging along Bayshore for three years." Thurber says between breaths. "Nobody's picked me up."

And then, almost out of earshot, the 33-year-old yells, "I wish they did!"

Source: *Tampa Tribune*, Aug. 3, 1995, with permission.

Index